About the author

Rajni Kothari is an internationally renowned
scholar and activist. He founded the Centre
for the Study of Developing Societies
(CSDS) and Lokayan (Dialogue of the
People). His previous publications include
the seminal works *Politics in India*, *Caste
in Indian Politics*, *Footsteps into the Future*,
State against Democracy and *Communalism
in India*.

Rethinking Democracy

RAJNI KOTHARI

Zed Books

LONDON | NEW YORK

Rethinking Democracy was originally published in 2005. This edition was published in 2007 by Zed Books Ltd, 7 Cynthia Street, London N1 9JF, UK and Room 400, 175 Fifth Avenue, New York, NY 10010, USA

www.zedbooks.co.uk

Published by arrangement with Orient Longman Private Limited

Cover photo copyright © Anand Balaji, 2007
<http://flickr.com/photos/anand_balaji>

Cover designed by Andrew Corbett
Set in Adobe Garamond
Printed in the EU by Biddles Ltd

Distributed in the USA exclusively by Palgrave Macmillan, a division of St Martin's Press, LLC, 175 Fifth Avenue, New York, NY 10010.

A catalogue record for this book is available from the British Library.
Library of Congress cataloging in publication data are available.

Not for sale in South Asia.

ISBN 978 1 84277 945 3 hb
ISBN 978 1 84277 946 0 pb

Contents

Preface

Over the last several decades I have had the opportunity to reflect intellectually and politically on the structures and processes of democracy in India, and on the broader trajectories of social and political change in diverse societies and political systems. I had a rather positive view of democracy in these diverse settings; of democracy being the means towards the creation of a benevolent society. In evolving such a perspective I sought to lay stress on the creation of a just social order and an overarching and holistic conception of a multilevel and pluralistic polity.

However, in recent times I have found myself getting increasingly concerned with the failure of democracy – not just as a political system, but of the democratic idea itself – in fulfilling the basic task of reaching out to people, especially those residing in the lower reaches of the social order. I began to feel increasingly uneasy with recent democratic developments.

It is to this growing contradiction that this book is addressed.

1

Introduction

We have entered a phase of human history when long-cherished ideals of liberty, equality and fraternity appear increasingly difficult to realise. The ideals themselves are no doubt worth pursuing, as are values such as social justice, individual freedom and the idea of a state that could liberate people from the shackles of both tradition and modernity. These ideals and values together provide humankind with a vision of an utopian social order—humane and just. But how do we translate this utopia into reality? For long it has been imagined that a 'democratic way of life' will provide humanity with the necessary framework – at once institutional and ideological – through which the utopia could be realised. It is only in recent decades that the faith in such an ideological-cum-institutional framework for 'delivering the goods' is being questioned. In particular, faith in the democratic way of life is being questioned. To address the theme of the prospects for democracy in India with a broad societal rather than just political perspective, we have to ask where is the country headed, what are the possibilities for enhancing individual freedom and moving towards collective goals of social justice and emancipation.

India is already undergoing a massive process of inner change, involving the very womb of its culture and civilisation—from the awakening of the inner self in each individual being, to the democratising of civil society as a whole. India is also experiencing an opening up of the polity and the state, both in respect of their inner constituents and in their relation to other cultures, nationalities and civilisations. India faces the challenge of not just pursuing a set of social and political ideals; a deeper and more comprehensive involvement is necessary—to engage in *acts of human imagination* for dealing with the vast diversity of situations facing it; to perceive the diverse goals facing the country as part of one large, religious order. Religion here should be seen as a pluralistic *and* monistic discipline of discovering oneself, one's community, one's spiritual essence. And through the discoveries one engages in tasks of social–political–moral transformation and emancipation. These tasks will extend the self all the way from inner intuitive drives to larger engagements in the sociopolitical arena, and further external involvements via-à-vis diverse nationalities, states and the globalising drives of transnational and corporate entities. Pluralism has been part of India's tradition and culture, inherent in its distinctive view of religiosity that draws inspiration from several faiths, but in large part from the Hindu cultural essence (even as Hinduism today faces grievous danger from the new ideology of hindutva and the accompanying mind-set as well as organisational ethos).

The challenges contemporary India faces are—how to relate and join the deeper, i.e. the inner, drives of citizens and communities to the broader challenge of sociopolitical transformation and the still larger challenge of emancipation; how to engage in the preservation of freedom and autonomy in the face of external confrontations of both corporate and transnational varieties, and confrontations found *within* the nation state, such as economic divides based on class and caste, and the more threatening communal and fundamentalist drives that are overtaking a vast variety of religious constellations, castes and communities.

Viewing Indian reality as it unfolds in our time: of all the domains impinging on contemporary India – from the personal to the considerable diversity characterising civil society, to that of the state and its political processes – it is the political that dominates. It penetrates all other domains. This politicisation applies as much to religion and caste as to the highly personalised domains of families, friendships and neighbourhoods, and close-knit circles of clubs, professional groups and peer groups. In the recent past it has been argued that religious loyalties and social structures are emerging as alternative foci to those more clearly political in nature. This is no longer the case. Following the collapse of hindutva and the L.K. Advani–led attack against 'pseudo-secularists' (the Bhartiya Janata Party (BJP) and the Sangh Parivar representing according to him the real secular entities) the reins of power were handed over to Atal Behari Vajpayee who in turn engaged in alliances with non-BJP politicians and groups, many of whom were committed (at least in their pronouncements) to the secular idea. Vajpayee's wooing of dalit, tribal and minority vote-banks, and the gradual sidelining of communal and religious ties with groups like the Vishva Hindu Parishad (VHP), the Rashtriya Swayamsevak Samiti (RSS), the Shiv Sena and the Bajrang Dal has been more political than religious. Though in the process, the Sangh Parivar groups have begun to form murderous facist gangs, fascism being the phenomenal distortion of the appeal of secularism in our time. With that, hindutva has also turned more militaristic.

With this distortion of Hinduism by hindutva, there is an atmosphere of growing alienation and intolerance between majority and minority communities. Even in other parts of the world, ruling structures are coming under the influence of strong-armed mafia and lumpen elements, accompanied by the rise of money power and growing criminalisation and corruption, producing anxiety about terrorism and the increasing influence of security and paramilitary forces. These are the ultimate consequences of perverse forms of politicisation of life, whether this be in the domain of civil society and the grassroots level at which rightwing groups are gaining ascendance (in place of left and liberal groups that had initiated the grassroots perspective), or in the arena of militant religious groupings and their search for omnipotence in place of what was once a pluralist framework. India's real misfortune lies in this hijacking of plural structures by monotheist and centripetal social and political ideologies. The same has happened in Sri Lanka, Pakistan, Bangladesh, Nepal, the rest of South Asia and beyond. The roles played by institutions of corporate capitalism – consisting on the one hand of Brettonwoods institutions like the World Bank, the International Monetary Fund (IMF) and other such global bodies, and on the other hand, the array of transnational corporations – have also contributed to the destruction of pluralism. A plethora of non-governmental organisations (NGOs) operating within individual countries, including so-called grassroots groups as well as the newly empowered party and party-like formations at decentralised levels are now being drawn into this vortex.

I have for long been a believer in the political process, its inherent dynamics, its capacity to correct imbalances and institutional erosions, its basic thrust towards empowering people, even those found in underprivileged and oppressed social terrains. Even today I want to work towards the restorative ethics of basic political process leading to ever-growing possibilities of *change*, indeed, the very idea of change, and the prospect of turning what is currently a crisis of change into a real challenge of change. This has to be done in the full spirit of transformative and emancipatory politics. Nothing outside of politics can do this, not even religion, despite its inherent humanising and service-oriented potentials. For religion to work towards change, or let us say for castes and communities to do this, they will need to develop discreet strategies for restoring pluralism- and diversity-enhancing possibilities. Religion is fast ceasing to be available for such restructuring. Caste still has the possibility for such restructuring, provided it is transformed in ways that lead to new realignments in the social structure starting from the bottom. Even traditional institutions of family and kinship, caste and community, are being subjected to churning, leading either to violence, or on the positive side, to a restructuring of the institutional framework of civil society. Underlying it all is the role of dissent at various levels, dissent being the operative core of the political process. Indeed, underneath the surface stillness, much is on the boil, only waiting to find institutional or societal expression.

For, the crux of real change lies in the bottom–up processes inherent in democratic politics that have as yet remained latent. Many of the new stirrings at the bottom indicate the growth of a new democratic process. A new revolution is unfolding leading to growing consciousness and political activism among the masses. New social formations are under way: class as a factor, producing fresh turbulences amongst castes and tribal groups; the rise of a new middle class in the form of other backward castes (OBCs) that own land and are relatively prosperous, even though they have been left behind in the social arena. Then there are new types of movements found to be growing among the women, the youth, the unemployed, the migrants—the whole spectrum of what can be called the underclass of history.

It is not as if throughout the post-independence era those who constitute the underclass were neglected. There was a long period when the Congress system was dominant, a system that encompassed a wide variety of internal adjustments between groups and factions. There were other manifestations of intra-party democracy as well. The role of Jawaharlal Nehru in cementing the internal dynamics of the Congress party needs to be borne in mind. It is only after the Emergency was imposed and a variety of post-Emergency trends emerged that politics became an instrument of dominant individuals and interests. There was a weak opposition while the so-called third system of parties and individuals simply did not manage to create an alternative to the Congress and the BJP. The V.P. Singh dream seems to have gone awry (although he did succeed in promoting the cause of the lower castes). Non-party political movements are lagging behind. Decentralisation of the panchayati-raj type has also, except in some regions, failed to bring about the desired change in the nature of the prevailing system. It has no doubt created some assertions at the grassroots and is currently beginning to spur demands in some areas for politics oriented towards self-rule. Taking advantage of the institutionalisation represented by panchayati raj through the two amendments of the Constitution of India, there have been further demands for expanding the base of self-rule, particularly from tribal communities that have begun asserting their need for autonomy at the political level and control over natural resources at the socioecological level. (This required yet another constitutional amendment.) There has also been a wide-ranging upsurge of the marginalised strata which resulted in a set of progressive measures spanning earlier provisions of reservations for the scheduled castes and scheduled tribes to the more recent adoption of the recommendations of the Mandal Commission benefitting the OBCs—all of this seeking to broaden the political base. Yet not much seems to have changed in the macro-arena, or for that matter even at the grassroots level. Even dalit assertions, first within the Congress and the Left parties and then in the framework of the party and parliamentary system as a whole, seem to be in the doldrums.

One of the more recent developments on the Indian scene has been the phenomenon of 'hung parliaments', given the fact that no party is able to achieve majority at the national level (and lately in some of the states as well). It is this aspect rather than any claims to democracy that has led to the growth of coalition governments. Thus the failure to create a non-Congress and non-BJP structure of power had ironically led to the BJP-led coalition of the National Democratic Alliance (NDA). The alliance drew on a vast array of regional parties and some highly personalised groupings which too, after a short period of seeming stability, began to show serious cracks. The basic flaw lies in the system of representative democracy following the western model, in turn based on the earlier notion of representation of interests, now taking the form of factions within the social terrain and the polity. It has in fact led to a dampening of the attempt to have more direct forms of democracy that were once sought to be introduced through various struggles like 'direct action'; the politics of self- determination fuelled by region-, class- and caste-based identities; and the growth of political competition in various local arenas. However, India seems to be in a state of continuing turmoil. The churnings at the ground level and the changes at the regional level are yet to aggregate into a workable macro-level alternative. There is a need to return to the earlier theme of argued inner change, evident in the new socioeconomic cravings among individuals and communities leading to grassroots politics, a phenomenon that challenges the representative model of democracy operating at the state and national levels.

Individuals are found to be experiencing new kinds of catharsis. These range from the psychological interfaces extending from the inner recesses to the still broader communitarian thrusts contributing to the ongoing catharsis of a more collective kind. I would expect the basic churnings that are or will be overtaking India to start with individual catharsis and move on to more collective manifestations, including those of the spiritual and para-religious kinds. They are far more important than the party/political kind which are more to be found on the surface. The real depths are provided by the social, psychological, spiritual and religious changes. India is in the throes of basic changes from within. No conception of the future will suffice that does not start with this key datum of Indian reality, i.e. recognition of the individual's psychological and spiritual impulses. It is indeed the key to grasping the essence of India.

No doubt the complacency of such a one-point analysis is unaffordable. It is not as if there are no immediate problems, or that they can be explained away by laying out such a preferred model, and all that matters is the future and we can leave the past and the present behind. On the contrary, a series of problems are staring us in the face. There is growing poverty, rising illiteracy, inequity, injustice and, in consequence, a considerable spurt in violence. The phenomenon of terrorism is a consequence of both the erosion of basic institutions and the undermining of the sociopsychological depths of the political process. I have made a conscious attempt to draw attention to what is basic to the understanding of the complex reality of India, for two reasons: First, merely describing in graphic detail without examining the causes, or simply predicting future scenarios without working out how they can be achieved will be of no help. Second, I continue to hold an optimistic view of India, despite all the stresses and strains that it may have to undergo in the process of drawing on the inner change.

In sum, India is now in the throes of a major turbulence. Changes are already taking place, though the basic social terrain is still stagnant. There is a need to think beyond the merely political and tap the deeper psycho-spiritual dimensions of Indian reality. That will help us gain a better understanding of the fast-changing Indian reality, than has been possible with our reliance on vague conceptions of democracy and democratic politics.

2

Democracy: In Search of a Theory

A broader perspective on the issues raised in the introduction will be provided in this chapter. We live in an age of democratic consciousness. Age-old hegemonies are being challenged or have crumbled. Ideological doctrines fashioned to perpetuate dominance and control are being widely questioned.

Recognition

It is not well recognised that we also live in an age of growing backlash and crushing onslaught against democratic forces; an age of cooptation of the voices of protest and intellectual dissent. New hegemonies are being configured and perpetuated. Widely held beliefs and deeply ingrained doctrines – of security, stability and unity – are being used to pursue patterns of governance that are clearly anti-democratic. It is even less clearly recognised that the very structures that had been conceived for promoting the democratic process and providing liberation from traditional constraints – political parties, representative institutions and the judiciary – are becoming vulnerable to the influence of anti-democratic forces. Democratic structures are proving incapable of dealing with these forces. There are some major exceptions to be found among the judiciary, the press and the intellectuals.

Perhaps the least recognised are the deep forces of erosion, uncertainty and anomie that are taking hold of the middle-class mind at a time when the vacuums created by the undermining of institutions and the decline of democratic temper are being filled by specialists in violence, corruption, private arms trade and gang warfare. All of which is leading to a sharp decline in the role of the political process set in motion by conscientious members of political parties and administrative services. Their ability to mediate social conflicts and restore faith in the democratic process among the people and the 'operators of the system' has been severely limited. The result has not just been political instability, but also a tendency to engage in activities that fragment and destabilise the social order. Disruptions in the functioning of the democratic system and a wide range of conflicts in the social arena have been the consequences of such erosion. The conflicts include social violence, the rise of negativist identities (communal and otherwise), and the growth of doctrines of exclusion and dispensability according to which entire populations are dismissed as unwanted.

Finally, the real actors and movements that have been struggling for the civil and democratic rights of various segments are being engulfed by new vulnerabilities of the communal or ethnic kind, or are being pushed out of public consciousness. As the public is overwhelmed by immediate issues of stability and survival, the challenges of economic survival, gender inequities, ecological destruction and human rights are neglected. Institutional channels that had been devised for dealing with these challenges are choked and all manner of narrow and selfish interests are exploiting state power.

Erosion

Central to this scenario of social and political erosion is the sharp decline in the legitimacy and authority of what was until recently considered the key institution of civil society—the modern state. Both the conception of the state as a negative good where authoritative assumption of disproportionate power was considered essential for providing order and security, and the more positive conception of the state as an instrument of liberation and transformation have suffered a decline in credibility.

There are many reasons for the erosion of the authority and legitimacy of the state. First, the erstwhile vision of making the state a condition for civilised existence has been under attack from two antagonistic forces—those who would subject every institution to the homogenising impulse of economic development and technology; and those who would insistently defend the autonomy of diverse cultures and identities. Pitchforked between these globalist and decentralist thrusts, the institutions of the state are found to be doubly vulnerable.

Second, a marked change has taken place in the growth of both leftwing and rightwing ideologies which have had a direct bearing on the role of the state. The leftwing perspective has moved from a statist conception of power for reordering society to a grassroots conception of rights for deprived classes, genders and environments. There has also been a change in the very conception of rights, with the colour having shifted from red to green. The rightist idea of making the state a defender of order and security in diverse national settings has given way to the principle of the market as the new integrative ideology at the global level. Once again the state is caught between globalist and localist pressures.

Third, a completely new set of interests has emerged in the public arena. There are global corporate interests arising from the latest phase of capitalism with transnational corporations as key factors. These interests are not merely economic and technological. For there are new extensions of the state and the corporate structure that are rooted in world militarisation, impinging on the nation state in the guise of providing it muscle.

At a deeper level, there are revivalist and fundamentalist pressures emanating from the social and cultural terrain that are also challenging the authority of the state. The traditional institutions of the state and polity – legislatures and courts, political parties and the bureaucracy – are unable to cope with these new and powerful interests and pressures.

Fourth, as the institutions of the state are overwhelmed by these opposing tendencies and interests, political leadership becomes increasingly uncertain of itself and gives way to catalysts of money and muscle power, negotiators of overt and covert deals, and commissions and kickbacks at the higher reaches of the state apparatus. As these become public knowledge the credibility of governing structures and ultimately of the state take a sharp plunge. The result is bewilderment commonly expressed in outbursts such as 'We do not know what is happening!' It is the average citizen's lack of comprehension that accounts for the current predicament of the state.

Reassertion

Despite the erosion of institutional spaces, in fact during the period of erosion, major assertions of people's rights have taken place from many vantage points. These range from class-based struggles against upper-caste and upper-class hegemonies to the struggle for women's rights, new assertions of peripheral and forcibly displaced communities against the destruction of their environments, tribal uprisings for safeguarding their locations and lifestyles, and strident defences of cultures, regional identities and nationalities. These assertions constitute a broad range of popular awakenings, protests and social movements. People's commitment to and faith in democratic values have been rising simultaneous to the decline of these values among the elite. The result is a marked transformation in the social basis of democracy, from the early liberal defence of incremental diffusion of institutional spaces to the more radical assertion of civil liberties and democratic rights. Paradoxically, most of these struggles and demands are directed at the state, the same state that is under attack from both global and local forces. The result is that the mass of the people are still committed to the state even though the state has fallen prey to interests that have no commitment to, or even compassion for, the people.

Increasingly shorn of its earlier autonomy from dominant interests, the state is proving incapable of responding to these various awakenings and movements, and unwilling to expand its own social base. Instead, it assumes confrontational postures vis-à-vis various sections of the people described by the media in terms of their caste, ethnicity and region, and branded by the ruling elites as extremist, anti-social and even anti-national. The perception of the state being subjected to challenges has increased; this perception is now used as a cover for repressive measures perpetuated by both agents of the state (police, paramilitary and armed forces) and agents of ruling juntas or parties (politicians, private armies of industrialists or landlords, and armed lumpens employed by dominant factions or communities).

It is this polarisation – between a state increasingly unwilling to carry out its constitutional obligations and a people not knowing who else to turn to – that is setting the stage for the growing incidence of violence, inequity, destruction of natural resources, contraction of institutional spaces and the consequent decline in more moderate and constructive modes of dissent. Two opposing tendencies have been set in motion as a result of this polarisation—a techno-managerial response from the elite (both governing and oppositional) and an ethnic (that is, communal, caste or religious) response from the diverse social peripheries. The 'crisis of the state' therefore enters a critical stage as it becomes increasingly difficult to find solutions to the diverse situations facing the state *within* its own framework.

Civil society also enters a critical stage and the tendency among diverse social strata to seek solutions outside the frameworks of the state and civil society grows. Meanwhile, just as a new breed of corporatism takes charge of the state, replacing the bureaucratic with the technocratic, a new breed of voluntarism takes root among the ethnic and religious minorities, deprived social groups and various non-amalgamated communities like the tribals and inhabitants of hills and forests. It is a type of voluntarism based on a combination of alienation from the state and assertion of exclusivist identities.

All these tendencies get heightened in plural and multiethnic societies like India. Here, democracy is expressed in and through a diversified social terrain while the state faces the task of restructuring its internal composition along lines that are quite different from those obtaining in western democracies. This accounts for the continuous stress on decentralisation and, as a step in the direction of decentralisation, on federalism. The advantage of a decentralised perspective is that it is conceived within the framework of the state, but is sensitive to the plurality of civil society. This perspective is as integral to the institutional model of democracy, just as it is an attempt to transform the nature of the state rather than give up on it.

We need a new theory of democracy that can comprehend the incapacity of existing institutional and ideological models, identify the reasons for this incapacity in a fast-changing global historical setting and provide a framework of active interventions at different levels of world reality to deal with an altogether new human agenda. At present we have no theory of democracy. The theory that emanated from the west (now defunct) was based on an inordinately atomistic view of both the individual and the state, a disproportionately homogenous conception of social and cultural reality, and was excessively influenced by the competitive ethos of bourgeois capitalism. Neither the socialist attempt to establish a welfare state nor the communist model of people's democracy have been able to cope with the new consciousness of the rights and dignities of diverse populations that has emerged all round the world, in particular, the third world. For the new consciousness cannot find fulfillment by merely focussing on the capture of state power, and the policies and programmes that the state should pursue. We need a democratic theory that accepts the great diversity of human situations and yet provides coherence to them through an active political process, and opens up new and creative spaces within the framework of civil society while simultaneously restructuring the state to realise these ends. The state and civil society have to deal with the issues in the relationship between the state and democratic process in a period of growing social turmoil and global managerial response. We need a theory of democracy that seeks to redirect the attention of intellectuals and social and political activists to the institution of the state; a theory that attempts to civilise the state and to make governance more humane than has been so far.

Such a theoretical stand becomes necessary as contemporary India is in a state of turmoil. Whereas there is widespread commitment to the democratic state in large sections of the society, we have to contend with the profound dislocations in the economic, technological and resource bases of the people, produced by the impact of the modern theory of development on the thinking of the elite. Every society must work on managing the profound consequences of modern science and technology, and the doctrine of development and theory of state that have emerged in their wake. It must deal with the fragmentation and centralisation inherent in the modernist world view, and preserve the integrity and inner vitality of its traditions, communities, lifestyles and values, while fully accepting the need for change and developing the capacity to cope with such change.

Reasons for Democracy

Democracy provides the impulse towards change, an impulse that is deeply ingrained in the Indian tradition and provides the leitmotif of its current awakening, engulfing large masses of the people and informing a wide array of social movements. The political process in India is informed by the struggle between the democratic process and the technocratic drives of the elite that militate against such popular aspirations. India is (still) democratic, but for it to stay democratic will depend on the outcome of the struggle being waged not just at the sociopolitical but also the intellectual and philosophical levels. The values and aspirations generated by this struggle run into serious obstacles arising not so much from structural or cultural impediments inherent in traditional society (as was presumed in much of comparative political theory till recently), but rather from the mindless pursuit of the modern development paradigm and the usurpation of community resources and lifestyles by the elite. This elite is keen to catch up with other societies than on working to provide equitable and humane conditions for its own people.

With the exception of 1975–76, how has India been able to remain democratic? Why, despite massive socioeconomic problems and the prolonged incapacity of governments to resolve them, has democracy not been undermined? How has the democratic polity not given way under increasing onslaughts from ethnic and regional separatist movements, the rise in religious fundamentalism and the persisting hold of illiteracy and poverty?

These questions are, no doubt, real and genuine. But in part they continue to be posed because of their misplaced theoretical simplicity—that there is an inherent antithesis between democracy and aspects like tradition, economic backwardness, strong parochial identities and low development indices of modernisation (literacy, urbanisation, exposure to mass media, and the spread of rationality and scientific values and temper). If we accept such a standardised conception of the essential 'prerequisites' of democracy, India is bound to be a deviant case, as has been argued from both the right and the left, in modern western thought. These arguments ignore the great relevance of tradition and culture to imparting depth and resilience to a democratic polity.

India is a deviant case in a much more fundamental sense— most threats to democracy in India arise from the sector that promotes modernity. The pursuit of state power by this sector crushes traditional pluralities in an effort to turn the country into a modern, united, prosperous and powerful economy and polity. The real threats come from the social strata that are found to be working for this 'modern' enterprise, from those very centres of power and expertise that are destabilising Indian traditions and the vast populace that is still steeped in those traditions. It is only because of the great appeal for large masses of the people of the very idea of democracy, and of the need to struggle for it, that the country continues to be democratic. Therefore, while India may suffer reverses and occasionally experience widespread civil strife or even an authoritarian backlash, its future as a democracy is assured.

3

The Democratic Polity: Philosophical and Cultural Perspectives

India is one of the few countries that had consciously chosen a democratic form of government and followed the choice with a series of progressive measures meant to empower the people. On examination it is clear that India has fallen short of realising what it had set out to achieve. It is the same state of affairs with many other countries claiming to be democracies. There has never been a time when democracy has not been at crossroads. As we move further into the twenty-first century, democracy has entered a period of prolonged crisis, with growing ambivalence about the specific goals that should be pursued. As a system of conducting human affairs, it is being viewed with increasing uncertainty.

Emerging Threats

The tremendous impact of technological power on the span and size of government and corporate organisations has shaken the earlier assumptions on which democratic polity was based. Centralisation of initiative, growth in the manipulative component of organisational behaviour at the expense of the participant component, and the growing institutional complexity in the management of power have all led to an increasingly corporate organisation of not just the economy but of the state as well.

The new economic framework of high capitalism, high technology and high affluence for the elite strata of society is the second major factor taxing the democratic polity. It is a framework in which a growing inflationary spiral has greatly escalated the cost of essential raw materials, agricultural inputs and energy, and consequently the cost of food, shelter and health. Internationally, this framework – whose basic features derive from the Euro-American lifestyle normative even in the vast peripheries of the globe characterised by massive poverty, unemployment and undernourishment – has resulted in growing competition for the distribution of scarce world resources. This problem is further confounded by the growing share of arms production and sale in the economic activity of major industrial nations, militarising their economies, and in turn militarising the nations of the third world. The acquisition of military hardware exported by the industrialised countries to the third world spells disaster for peace in the latter regions. Militarisation strains the capacity of the third world people to resist the oppression and genocidal acts perpetrated by their governments. The short-term economic revival of industralised societies identified as democracies may be assisted by arms production on an unprecedented scale, but it can only undermine the fine balance on which their democratic and pluralist polities have all along rested, and at the same time produce an external environment which will destroy the balance of the international order, in particular, third world polities and cultures.

Long-term Trends

Threats to the survival of democratic polity have arisen not only due to recent developments in the secular arrangements in the domestic and international spheres. They are also the consequence of a basic conflict in the *weltanschauung* of the modern world which can be traced back to the evolution of the west, starting with the Renaissance, crystallising in the Enlightenment, and flowering in the age of the Industrial Revolution and modern capitalism.

If we examine the malaise that has overtaken humanity in recent times – organised and accelerating violence, decline in human empathy and compassion, growth of exploitation and cruelty, coexistence of corrupting affluence and dehumanising misery – we are forced to take a hard look at the peculiar world view and philosophy of life, modernity, that first evolved in western societies and has since spread throughout the world.

In general, the history of western society constitutes the struggle to discover a viable social and political order with a view to minimise the capriciousness of nature, and the solitariness and inherent brutality of man ('man' here represents all that is human). This has been the concern of almost all influential thinkers of the west, despite the Socratic concern with virtue and Pascal's counsel against unlimited rationalism. What has mattered most in western thinking is how to evolve a perfect, good, beneficent and affluent society. As there was inherent evil in man that resulted in strife and in wars, it was necessary to not view the great expressions of the human mind as ends in themselves, but as means in the creation of an efficient society free from strife, violence, arbitrariness and unpredictability. Hence the need not only to discover the laws of nature and subject nature to human control but also, as with Hobbes, to discover the laws of human nature and to subject its vagaries to covenants governing all men. Or alternatively, as with Hegel and Marx, to uncover the laws governing history and realise the progressive principles in history that are at once desirable and inevitable.

Such a view of man's place in the universe has generated a powerful sense of man's mastery over nature. Knowledge of the laws of nature has become an important condition of human freedom. The model of scientific cognition and manipulation of the environment has been applied with equal force to human nature and its potentiality, to the building of social and political institutions, and to the conquest of time itself.

In spite of the sense of mastery over nature and the confidence in building an efficient social order, however, modern man's capacity to relate himself to the universe is limited in two major areas. The first involves man and his ability to exercise control over his desires and passions. Although modern biology and psychology have made some spectacular advances in laying bare the process of human evolution, it appears as if the very instruments of domination and control that modern man has perfected vis-à-vis his environment have taken on a Frankensteinian quality and made him the prisoner of his own achievements. Science and industry – the presumed agents of human liberation – have been transformed from being the means to self-realisation, to being ends in themselves.

The second limitation of modern man's cognitive capacity involves the very relationship between man and nature that has been the main concern of science. Modern man is in continuous tension with nature. The relationship is based not on an integral view of nature but, rather, on one of manipulation of external objects that become instruments of man's power and righteousness. This is a serious shortcoming in the phenomenological perspective that underlines both modern science and modern philosophy. The divorce between science and morality informs this perspective. The axiology of the latter still falls outside the scope of science. Reason, the principal instrument of scientific method, is limited to the arena of empirical truth in the cognitive sense and has not yet been extended to cover the fields of ethics and aesthetics. Given this limitation, the challenge of evolving an integrated human consciousness remains unresolved. This is the basic weakness of the scientific world view, as it has developed so far.

Immanuel Kant's characterisation of western humanism with the belief of each man being an end in himself, led in time to the idea of free will and to a gradual separation of the world of values from the world of nature. Underlying this schism is the splitting of the human psyche into isolated components of cognition and connation, and in turn the separation of law from the entities of which it is a law. The concept of free will thrived on such a separation and in secular life gave rise to the meaningless problem, first posed by Plato, of uniting the philosopher and the king.

Such a separation between man and nature, body and mind, intellect and feeling, has produced a mental climate of arrogance. Man in his position of command does not find the need to view his relationship to the rest of existence as constituting an organic whole. The most striking evidence of this thinking can be seen in the manner in which the findings of Charles Darwin were used for social and philosophical ends. Instead of heeding Darwin's central thesis on the animal origins of man, and his demonstration of the basic unity and continuity in the evolutionary process, his nineteenth-century interpreters were more impressed by the concepts of natural selection and survival-of-the-fittest that appeared to establish man as a superior being. This interpretation has been challenged in recent times but the mind-set to which it gave rise continues to persist.

The mind-set persists in the third world too. The gospel of modernisation – based on a package of urbanisation, achievement motivation, mass media exposure, specialised education, spatial mobility and a rising consumption of finished goods – that has overtaken and intoxicated the westernised middle class in the third world, has been the principal vehicle of contemporary processes of economic expansion, cultural domination and political hegemony. Its universalising credo is deeply affecting the autonomy of individual human beings, diverse cultures and most nations as well. It has shaken the self-respect of peoples, made them feel ashamed of their own traditions, and has given rise to a high degree of ambivalence in their relationship to their own societies.

New Class Ethos

It is necessary that we understand the class ethos emerging in modern society all over the world. Capitalism, socialism and social democracy in most countries of the world are being increasingly defined by a middle-class elite that has adopted the model of a technocratic state in which political, industrial and military power are concentrated. It is significant that the economic ethic underlying capitalism has undergone a major shift. Capitalism no longer depends on the habits of thrift and saving that were highlighted in the conception of the Protestant ethic. It now relies on a diametrically opposite economic ethic, the ethic of constant want and waste, that is necessary to keep the industrial machine and its managerial edifice functioning. It is also significant that communism where it has survived has also changed its original rationale of freeing human beings from the reified constraints of wage labour, class and the state, to demonstrating technological power and industrial efficiency.

Almost in every part of the globe there has been a growth in the manipulative component of the modern state and its industrial mainstay, both of which are dominated by bureaucrats and professional managers. These groups have firm command in the developing countries too, partly because they are in control in the metropolitan centres. The technocrats of the world operating from command positions form a class of their own. In this situation the role of politics as an exercise of options by ordinary human beings – for freedom, equality and a classless society – is contracted by the concentration of power among a few. This was inherent in the hedonistic world view that assumed charge of modern man and his productive apparatus in the last hundred and fifty years. Therefore, the great advances of modern science and technology have only succeeded in reiterating the elementary problem of human survival—now on a world scale and with the aid of instruments of mass destruction. A war with nuclear weapons or a collapse of the environment may annihilate a large part of the human race.

The Role of Knowledge

Central to this model of life and the class formations it has originated across the world is the role of knowledge in human affairs. Never before had the product of the human mind acquired so dominant a role in the shaping of societies as in modern times. It has changed the world beyond recognition. Its basic contribution has been to give man a tremendous sense of power and the capacity to manipulate. Nothing else could have made man – especially the educated man – so arrogant as this particular role of knowledge. And it has made the purveyors of this knowledge, in collusion with the users of this knowledge, a class in themselves.

It is not that knowledge by itself has brought humanity to grief. The rise of modern science has been a great liberator of man from the horrors of nature and of religious doctrine. But the original promise of the progress of science has been undermined. Because science flourished in a culture (viz. of the west) that looked upon it as an instrument of power and domination rather than as a liberator of the human spirit – knowledge as perceived by the ancient Chinese, the Indians and the Greeks – it soon became an instrument of technology. Not content with overcoming hardships and fulfilling basic needs, technology was used for continuous expansion, competition and domination. It became an instrument of monopoly and inequality with the fruits of technology diffused widely within some societies at the expense of a great many other—societies which actually provided the raw materials for the prosperity of the few.

In sum, because of a particular cultural location where modern technology flourished it has become Frankensteinian in character. The myth that modern technology had given rise to has suddenly exploded—the myth of perpetual progress, of end to scarcity, and of infinite progress accessible and available to all. Today, suddenly the affluent world faces the consequences of the excesses of modern technology; see for example, the animated discussion on environmental crises.

However, the environmental crisis is only a symptom of a basic change in relationship—from man's reliance on nature to man's dependence on machines. The domination of man by the machine, and his dependence on it for his sustenance, means not just the constant and continuous need for energy and raw materials; it also entails less and less need for people. The world now has millions of 'marginal' men and women for whom society has no use. Man has become superfluous and obsolescent; he is being perceived as a burden not just on nature but also on society. Paradoxical though it may sound, man is the most dispensable element in the system that modern man has produced.

The crisis faced by modern man has been wrought by a particular direction that science and technology took under the impact of the age of positivism. The full consequences of such a course are seen in our time as it envelops all the crises to which scientists and philosophers have drawn our attention—the threat of total war, of the extreme dualism of a world so divided that its very survival is at stake. It is not certain that such a badly divided species can survive the increasing states of tension and violence that it will have to face. Many other species that have confronted such conditions have perished, and none of them had possessed the man-made instruments of destruction.

Rethinking the Human Enterprise

The need to rethink the general premises of both the liberal state and the democratic polity through which it functions, is now widely recognised. Unless such rethinking takes place in the larger context of the contemporary human condition, it is not likely to succeed in creating a relevant political context in which intellectuals can find their bearings. It is necessary to relate the realm of politics to the realm of science. There is a definite need to critically review the philosophical world view which has made science an instrument of secular power, and in consequence has given rise to a specific class configuration at great variance with the assumptions of both classical liberalism and theoretical Marxism.

There is need to move beyond both the liberal and marxist world views, both of which are offshoots of eighteenth-century European Enlightenment and nineteenth-century mechanistic humanism. Those like John Rawls have nobly argued for rescuing the liberal doctrine from hedonistic and positivistic streams of thought; a rescue that is unrealisable. For liberalism contained the seeds of its own demise in being closely interwined with the theory of infinite progress and the paradigm of science and techno-economic development. Marxism, the principal critique of liberalism, has also suffered from the same basic inadequacies despite the early Marx who was deeply concerned with issues of human alienation and commodity fetishism. These early writings of Marx were resuscitated by Lukacs and his followers in Hungary and elsewhere, and further developed and reformulated by members of the Frankfurt School like Habermas and reformers within the marxist school like Gramsci—all of which have since been relegated to memory.

All these attempts, as well as critical writings of thinkers like Marcuse, can provide leads in reconsidering the basic liberal–marxist framework of modern democracy, but basic work on the whole paradigm of modernity, focussing on the issues outlined above is still necessary. Not only do we find the liberal and marxist frameworks unable to deal with the consequences of the modern industrial state and its international ramifications; we also find that we have, in the last hundred years or so, entered a new phase of politics at both national and global levels which challenge human intelligence afresh. Elsewhere in this book, where the very idea of democracy is critiqued, we will attend to various facets of this larger challenge to human aspirations.

We have looked at the role of knowledge in the arrangement of human affairs and the shaping of societies. In rethinking the democratic model it becomes obligatory to rethink the paradigm of science, especially that of the social sciences. The close relationship between free scientific inquiry into the structure of reality and the existence of democratic polity does not need to be argued. Social sciences especially, whether in respect to empirical research or normative questioning, cannot thrive except in democratic societies. Thorough investigation of the modes of conducting research, and financial and institutional support for it is likely to sensitise us to the perils that certain types of thinking and research, and their utilisation pose to democracy. Just as good social sciences can best thrive in an open society and democratic polity, the efficacy of a democratic polity and respect for it in the world at large depends vitally on the quality and integrity of its social sciences.

Social Sciences

It is now well known how certain schools of thought in American social sciences have gravely compromised the autonomy and dignity of the individual, and indeed of entire societies. The overall substantive result of American social scientists' involvement in the conduct of American foreign policy – in Southeast Asia, Latin America and among the Gulf nations – are not very different from the role of their counterparts in the former Soviet Union. Similar results have been produced by the 'committed intellectuals' of India. In thinking about the future it is important to consider the ethical dimensions of the involvement of researchers and research institutes in the shaping of public policy and through it the structure and ideological contours of modern states as well as civil societies.

Apart from such overall considerations of research policy, it is necessary to review certain fields of scholarship in order to arrest the tendency of professional pundits arrogating to themselves the role of being the arbiters of socioeconomic, political and administrative systems. Certain branches of the scientific estate – management science, systems research, science policy, certain branches of economics and public administration, foreign policy analysis and area studies – are particularly prone to this type of distortion in the relationship between experts, policy-makers and the general citizenry. Many of these branches have lost their moorings in basic disciplines and have established themselves as pseudo-disciplines with claims to special status as applied sciences. Without belittling the importance of certain fields of applied research, it is necessary not to make a fetish of the now-fashionable doctrine of relevance. The doctrine of relevance and these fields of applied research must be prevented from becoming the means to conformity apropos the wishes of governments and transnational corporate entities.

A final observation: There is much greater need than has been recognised so far, for pursuing theoretical research on ideas, principles of organisation and institutional structures, including fundamental critiques of these systems at both national and global levels. For, whether we like it or not, we have arrived at a point in human history where the real need, even from the point of view of good and relevant action, is for good and relevant theory. Work on such theory should be viewed as an integral part of exploring alternative modes for the realisation of basic democratic and civilisational values, distancing ourselves from the emerging penchant for straitjacketing diversities into an uniform mould and the consequent reliance on expertise for realising social goals. The survival and sustenance of the democratic polity, in the context of a fundamentally altered human condition, depends crucially on a reorientation of the educational process, both its theoretical postulations and the applications thereof; in particular, the role of social science expertise in arranging human affairs.

4

The Two Faces of Democracy: The Classes and the Masses

Focussing on the educational process and the role of the social sciences, specifically in enabling the lower reaches of society to engage in the politics of transformation, we are reminded that while we live in an age of turbulence, particularly at the grassroots, little seems to be changing in the world at large. I propose to explore precisely this contradiction—between an increasingly defensive status quo at the macro-level and the forces of change and transformation in a variety of micro-settings that are getting more and more restless. Though the latter remain disorganised and hence are unable to cope with the growing repression and backlash from the upper reaches of the system representing the macro-dimensions.

Such explorations have been undertaken at least since the middle of the nineteenth century. All social commentators, who have cared to look at the larger dynamics that lie behind the myriad expressions of the human condition have encountered deep ambivalence and uncertainty about what really is happening with the status quo at the global, regional and local levels, and with the agents of change and transformation from the local micro-levels to the global and planetary macro-levels.

Growing Uncertainty

It is only by seeking to unravel this deep uncertainty about the direction in which the world is moving – both the dominant structures and those opposed to them – that we may be able to begin unravelling what is at work, and on that basis comprehend the future of democracy. What are the new factors that have emerged and how are these likely to shape the future? What, if any, are the counter-trends? At present no clear framework of understanding, far less of explaining, reality exists. Ideological frameworks and grand theories have turned obsolescent, and there is no clear guide for formulating praxis. There has been a striking decline in confidence among all but the most naive dogmatists. This pervading sense of uncertainty has given rise to feelings of insecurity, helplessness, bewilderment, withdrawal, cynicism and apathy—all of high relevance to the future prospects of democracy.

We see uncertainty permeating many levels of human endeavour. Firstly, at the level of the world power structure the rise of the third world in the postcolonial period, the replacement of a Europe-centred world by a bipolar world dominated by two superpowers and then the post–cold war unipolar structure of global hegemony have unsettled all earlier understandings of international relations. While these two developments in contemporary history are recognised, the two have not been considered together in an adequate manner. Once that is done, we can see how colonial bondage has been replaced by a much greater and stronger integration into the global capitalist market and the strategic straitjacket fashioned by the struggle for world hegemony. Existing conceptual categories of historical analysis are inadequate to grasp the full implications of this split in the human community occasioned, in fact, by its greater integration fuelled by globalisation and homogenisation. Most existing ideologies and their offshoots were born in the typical European setting of nation states, which was also the setting of first-generation industrialisation and of essentially class-based identities. They seem to be ill-equipped to deal with the reality we face today—a transnationalised world with technology rather than economy or politics functioning as the dominant currency.

Secondly, the uncertainty is also reflected at the level of the organisation of the productive forces. We are confronted with a completely different mode of world capitalism, a switch from the European to the American model, in which technology as a system, particularly communications and information dimensions, is conditioning the behaviour of states, making all other relations of production subsidiary. This has forced all other systems – the socialist system, the state-sponsored mixed economy in the third world, the Japanese system – to fall in line. Success is now measured in terms laid out by the American cultural syndrome with its overriding emphasis on technology.

Thirdly, the growing autonomy and power of the technological estate has found its greatest manifestation in military affairs and military–civilian relationships. We live in an age not just of the growing militarisation of the globe but also of a model of militarisation that is essentially technological. Nation states are coming under the spell of military research and development (R&D) which marches inexorably and forces every country to discard existing weapons systems and adopt ever-new ones, at escalating costs. Weaponisation also has hazardous effects on social and ecological systems. It is a new version of militarism, largely autonomous of the will of the rulers and, of course, of the people.

Fourthly, this dominion of technology and its pervasive impact on political, economic and security dimensions – each of which has become vulnerable to the technological paradigm – has in turn produced a massive erosion of the ecological basis of human civilisation, destroying the resource base of the people, especially the millions of rural, tribal and ethnic poor. The latter have not just been rendered surplus and treated as dispensable populations by the aggressive march of high-tech capitalism. Even their traditional access to natural resources and non-commercial produce has been taken away from them. The resources of nature and heritage of history that were traditionally available freely to these people are now being siphoned.

The Dominant Ideology

As traditional societies are compelled to adopt the dominant ideology of forced modernisation and supposedly independent states too are similarly forced, a deep sociocultural crisis ensues; especially as the state surrenders its autonomy, and civil society has to fall back on its own resources. These societies are already experiencing deep convulsions as a result of two powerful impacts: first, the aggressive thrust of ruthless technologism, the new form that world capitalism has assumed; second, the social and ethnic conflicts generated by formal electoral democracy in which wresting a majority somehow has become the main focus. The use of the formal apparatus of democracy as a vehicle of modernisation worked smoothly so long as it was controlled by an alliance of feudal and bourgeois elements. With the rise and assertion of the masses which had in good faith believed in the formal pretences of bourgeois democracy, the feudal land-owning interests and the industrial bourgeoisie orchestrated a backlash. This has found expression in the massive repression of the poor, on the one hand; and on the other hand, the promulgation of a depoliticised technocratic state that is impervious to the social and political aspirations of the masses.

We need to comprehend and assess the bewildering interface between these powerful trends, each heralding a strong current of domination and destruction. Crucial to such an understanding are two prerequisites. First, we should give up the specialised, single issue-oriented approach to problems and crises that has characterised the natural sciences and the social sciences. Second, we need to identify the emerging ideological contours in the current thinking of the counter-movements. Both have to be merged to form a whole that draws upon the best in earlier ideologies, and empowers the masses towards a liberating process of their own creation and volition. If this is to be an 'age of the masses', then it is the masses and their leaders who have to evolve a relevant ideology, not intellectuals or the wielders of state power. The latter indicate a declining interest in the masses, except to mobilise them from time to time for their own perpetuation and glorification. Hitherto, ideological claims or pretences have been made either by intellectuals in their role of being vanguards or by governments or political leaders in control of the state; both have patronised the masses as mindless followers with no capacity for cognition. The elites, including those claiming to be revolutionary, have failed to grasp reality. On the other hand, refreshing and original ways of thinking are evident among the masses, from whom all of us can learn.

The Changing Nature of the State

The need to consider the multiple dimensions of domination, exploitation and marginalisation in their interrelated manifestations, and to similarly interrelate the large variety of counter-trends and their ideological underpinnings, can be best met by working on the one central issue of our times—the changing nature of the state and its role in civil society, especially as it impinges on the people of the third world. We need to reexamine our assumptions about the state and its presumed role as liberator, equaliser, moderniser and mobiliser. As we examine, we will be able to see that the state's relationship to the people is not just a series of interactions between the classes and the masses, but also between the principal carriers of modern capitalism and technology, and the social order; between the military and the civil orders; between the development policies of the state and its transnational sponsors, and the economic and ecological catastrophes threatening the survival of many; between the global information order and the citizens reduced to packages of consumption, social prejudice, and the dazzling circuses organised by agents of the state and corporate entities; and finally, between dominant races and ethnic entities that are in control of the state and those that are at the periphery. Those in the periphery are still members of the civic order, but are being pushed out by the repressive and genocidal policies pursued by the state and transnational entities. It is this capture of the state by a convergence of class, ethnic, technological and military actors, by developmentalists, communicators and managers that has set the stage for the confrontation between them and the people—between the classes and the masses.

In the postcolonial world (starting with the various national movements), the state is perceived as a mediator ameliorating the harshness of traditional social structures for the purpose of ensuring justice and equality, as a protector of the vulnerable social strata, and as a liberator of the oppressed and colonised populations. The state was to be an engine of growth and 'development' that would usher in a new civic order based on progress and prosperity. On the basis of the resources that were generated through such growth, the state would to be able to confer rights to life and liberty, equality and dignity, on the people at large. There was a further presumption of the relative autonomy of the state from entrenched interests and classes, of the state as an independent actor with preponderant powers to influence, discipline, and, where needed, coerce established interests and estates, making them accept new policies aimed at transforming the status quo. For a while it did seem that the bearers of power in the new states meant to act autonomously through the constitution and social legislation. The ensuing pursuit of economic models, whether in achieving greater self-reliance through import substitution and the building of a substantial infrastructure for industrialisation (for example, India), or in achieving greater welfare through provision of social minima in food, health and education (for example, Sri Lanka), was meant to enable the state to be a positive entity, governing on the basis of clearly laid-out policies built on a given social and economic philosophy.

During the same period, the opening out of political spaces – either through an exercise of adult franchise in liberal polities; or through involvement in party structures and at production sites in more socialist polities; or through a combination of competitive politics, local self-government and cooperatives in rural areas, in mixed economies – meant that leaders of these states were keen on involving the masses and seeking legitimacy from them. In turn, large segments of the masses accepted this benevolent form of the paternalistic state, and hoped to use it to improve their life chances and their status in society. Though not always stated, built into the positive thrust and progressivist creed of the postcolonial state was an eventual encounter between the classes and the masses, with the state providing a framework through which what appeared to be a clash of interests became the catalyst of a series of transformative policies.

The promise of a liberal polity through a mixture of faith in development, zeal in doing good to the people, and the availability of a credible and exemplary leadership not shackled by a particular class was not without failings. It also had its share of serious critics. Many compromises were made along the way, for instance, in pursuing land reforms or instituting truly effective public distribution systems. Concessions were made when entrenched groups and interests resisted intended changes. There was too much dependence on the bureaucracy which in most of these states was a direct continuation of the colonial civil service. And finally, there was corruption in high office given the inevitable compulsions of the middle-class basis of the leadership and the social milieu which both ministers and their secretaries, and technocrats inhabited.

We had been warned that the state was an instrument of a class that got its initial impetus from serving under the colonial power. And yet, whether it was Lenin or Mao, Nehru or Nkrumah, Nyerere or Nasser, they all pinned their visions of transformation on state power. Only Gandhi did not, but he was, even before India became independent, rendered impotent and irrelevant. Leaving aside the Gandhian stream (and most Gandhians also went for a model of voluntarism and constructive work which depended heavily on state patronage), there was consensus across the board, from industrialists to left-of-centre politicians and radicals (including the marxists), on the conception of a positive and interventionist role for the state—on behalf of the masses.

It is now clear that the expectation based on the state's role and the presumed alliance between the state and the people, have been belied. Today the state is seen to have betrayed the masses. It has become available to the dominant classes and their transnational patrons in pursuit of their interests, and has turned anti-people. Nor has the state provided the sinews of a bourgeois capitalist transformation from the evolution of which a revolutionary alternative would emerge. The state in the third world, despite some valiant efforts by dedicated leaders in a few countries, has degenerated into a technocratic machine serving a narrow power group that is held afloat by a widely entrenched bureaucracy and a hand-picked security apparatus, assisting in a regime of order and repression. It is kept functioning by millions of hardworking people who must continue to produce goods and services for the system, for if they did not, everything would collapse. Without landless labourers and sharecroppers, and the unrelieved drudgery of women and children, the rural economy would collapse; and without the availability of slum- and pavement-dwellers the urban economy would collapse. But none can rise above their penury and destitution—the landless cannot acquire land nor can the homeless urbanites get homes. On the contrary, the opposite could happen: their sinking below existing poverty levels in the wake of increase in unemployment following further modernisation; and the bulldozing of settlements, given the growing sentiment against migrant labourers without whom cities cannot be built, but who are an eyesore to the affluent strata. Sections of the middle classes too get affected by the onward march of this techno-managerial system, the lower strata among them getting pauperised through the unemployment and ruthless competition unleashed by the system.

Decline of the State and Rise of the Classes

The transformation of the state's role in the postcolonial world, from being an instrument of liberation of the masses to being a source of their oppression, is the result of a number of factors. Some of these were foreseen by theoretical models of historical change that were perceived even during the struggle for independence, but many others are a result of developments that were not foreseen, at least not adequately.

One set of factors has to do with the very model of development that was adopted in most postcolonial countries. Based on the urge to emulate and catch up with the countries that had once colonised them and from where their intellectuals continued to derive their main stimulus and sustenance even after independence, the development model produced a structure of opportunities that was inherently inequitous and pitched against the mass of the people. With the emphasis on capital accumulation for rapid industrialisation and the outward-looking understanding of industrialisation, urbanisation and modernisation (from the villages to the metropolitan centres), resources were distributed unevenly. These were resources not just created by planned economic development but also those that originally belonged to the people, or to which they had free and easy access. Initially these inequalities and disparities – between classes or regions, or those occasioned by the destruction of forests and other biospheres – were considered transitory, due to the inevitable lag between accumulation and distribution, and that they will not only disappear with further development but will be reversed in favour of the poor and towards a more egalitarian society. In reality, despite a degree of welfare measures that were adopted and despite a mixed technological package that included schemes for rural development meant to benefit the poor and unemployed, the pattern of inequalities and the nature of economic growth that promoted the inequalities have acquired a *structure* that has more or less become permanent and has given rise to many vested interests.

The reasons for the establishment of such a structure are many. There is the greed of the classes that controlled or had access to state power and administration at different levels, and who were unwilling to make the so-called sacrifices that would allow the poorer classes to gain access to the surplus that they had created in the first place. The typical liberal-bourgeois democratic assumption that sharing of surplus would help the whole society move forward, by benefiting all classes, has not worked in highly divided societies where the 'classes' and the masses constitute two different worlds.

But it was not simply a matter of greed, selfishness and lack of empathy for others among the upper classes. More basic was the absence of a larger perspective on how better distribution would lead to even greater enlargement of the surplus, instead of the narrow view of first enlarging the surplus because there isn't enough to distribute—a perspective in which growth and accumulation get *prior* attention. But these very lacks, of empathy and social perspective, were caused by other pressures.

At the level of individuals and groups of the owning classes, there was the snare of an imported package of consumption, amenities and lifestyle, which made for a highly seductive model of development. The American mass culture of consumption acquired a global outreach; in the case of societies of the third world, it became an elite culture that kept the masses out or moved them to the margins.

Having created an adequate industrial infrastructure that could generate enough surplus to satisfy the consumer needs of the top owning classes and their middle-class cohorts, through the institutions put in place by the state, the elite have lost interest in continuing the operation of an interventionist state. For that would mean responding to the demands of the classes lower down the social terrain, leading to pressures for redistribution, welfare and a more participatory framework of economic management. The result has been an emphasis simultaneously on liberalisation and lowering of taxes on the rich, presumably to increase incentives and replace the role of the state with that of the market, and on modernisation and computerisation of the technological base in which the state is expected to play a big role. While the classes (that is, the upper and middle classes) wallow in the imported mass culture of consumption and comforts, the masses themselves are pushed out into the unorganised sector. As for the organised sector of the economy, its attempt to get modernised for effectively competing in the export-led model of development, has given rise to a global mind-set that has produced a new clientele for international financial institutions, and an international academic and policy-making elite that has become at once client and consultant to such world bodies. It is all part of the catching- up syndrome—in consumption patterns, in technology and in the ruling doctrine about the best path to economic affluence.

The Catching-up Syndrome

The second set of factors, the more powerful set, responsible for the transformation of the state's role involves the catching-up process that has been at work. The process is driven by the desire to build an efficient, strong, heavily industrialised state that is sufficiently militarised, for which the latest and most sophisticated armaments are acquired. At the scent of such thinking transnational salespersons, experts in the latest civilian technologies and the merchants of violence, war, repressive technologies and intelligence systems moved in, laying out both their hardware and software. This mirage of greatness in a world increasingly dominated by one superpower and multinational corporate entities only serves to drain resources from the countryside to urban areas, and from there to abroad—in return for both civilian and military high-tech. It is a model that has increased areas of tension as the phenomenon of regional overlordship became an integral part of the structure of global management. It has also hardened the arteries of the state which found it necessary to suppress challenges locally in order to deal with external challenges. All of this has been inherent in the very logic of a global order based on technocratic and militarising states. As far as the masses of these states were concerned, the processes described here siphon the economic resources that could have been available for their well-being and, worse, siphon natural resources to which they had had access and of which the new technologies are particularly destructive.

Whither Welfare State?

Thirdly, as a consequence of these factors – the greed of the upper classes, particularly under the impact of modern consumerism; the catching-up syndrome; the drive towards a hard, efficient and militarised state; and above all the growing faith in market economies – we are witness to another important development that is happening now and is bound to accelerate. This is the rapid erosion of the welfare state and those components of development that were directed to the amelioration and welfare of the underprivileged. We need to remember that one of the more progressive streams in modern economic thought, within the broad liberal-bourgeois framework, has been the effort to chasten the harshness of modern capitalism and technology through the welfare state. The welfare state has proved to be a major defence of the capitalist order against radical and revolutionary forces, and yet it seeked to protect the mass of the people from the innate harshness of the capitalist order. When postcolonial states designed their models of development, they included welfare components of modern economic thought. Now with the welfare state under attack everywhere (including in the west, even in countries that had provided high levels of social security) those components have been the first to suffer in the third world. Belief in the market and in technological solutions to social and political problems has taken their place. Unlike in highly urban societies that were gradually industrialised where the growth of a strong class consciousness led to demands for equity and justice which emerged as pressures on the state, in predominantly rural and tribal societies, the state becomes a direct, unmediated presence. Whether such a state treats its citizenry humanely or oppressively depends on the adopted model of development, as well as on the balance of sociopolitical considerations that informs the model. The adoption of the model and the considerations informing it has depended substantially on the ruling elite. When such an elite makes a direct jump to high-tech without having gone through the dynamics of capitalist growth, and when it allows full play to military, tourism, television and information technology, the welfare component of development is ignored.

Once this happens both capitalism and the state get hardened, the state becoming an instrument of capitalism instead of softening its excesses. The state gives in to the compulsions of this computerised phase of capitalism—automation in the organised sector and a new division of labour in the unorganised sector with migrant and bonded labourers, and women and children becoming targets of exploitation. This phase destabilises the working class and its organisations. Their capacity to combat poverty, marginalisation and destitution – and slow death – declines as these very aspects become integral to the growth of the system and to the idea of science and therefore modern civilisation.

The New Emerging Mix

Fourthly, a new ideology has crystallised, engaging leaders and intellectuals in all parts of the world (including, to some extent, the former socialist world). The crux of the new ideology is breathtakingly simple: replacement of the state by the market. It is mainly built on the rightwing critique of a positive and interventionist state, while also drawing on the left–liberal attack on the greatly increased power of the bureaucracy. The market is euphemistically called 'free market', elements such as competition, modernisation and technology, and the transnational corporate giants are left unbridled. This doctrine is promulgated by the state and the new bearers of its power (that is, the post-Fabian generation). The basic idea is to dismantle the state apparatus in regard to distribution of the national produce, and yet fully and systematically use the same state apparatus to promote the new technologies and the dual economy that accompanies them. There has been movement towards the idea of a state that bears a human face, uses liberal symbols and invites everyone to join in, especially voluntary organisations and the non-governmental organisations, opposition groups and the liberal intelligentsia. It is a new injunction altogether: reduce the role of the bureaucracy, depoliticise the government and administration, and draw motivated and highly educated people into this great march forward on the basis of free market economy. The state is still central to this forward movement, for it is the state that is to drive us all as a homogeneous mass into the future. This is part of a grand strategy that calls for corporate collaborations. We are witness to the rise of a new model of the state – the corporate capitalist state – behind whose new look lurks the structure of corporate capitalism. All over the Association of Southeast Asian Nations (ASEAN) world and in the so-called newly industrialising countries (NICs) marriage of state and corporate capitalism has taken place; not just between the local bourgeoisie and foreign capital as earlier. In fact, local businesses were wiped out wherever corporate capitalism grew in strength.

The most dangerous element in this growing crystallisation of the ruling class is the stirring of communal passions. Aware that the dual economy and the social consequences thereof are likely to generate restlessness and revolt from the lower tiers of society and the politicised members of the middle classes, a new canard has been set in motion. It is meant to detract attention from the socioeconomic sphere. Public opinion and people's emotions are being directed towards the highly volatile communal and ethnic spheres. This has released strong religious, linguistic and cultural sentiments; pitched people against people; utilised mafia operations; and unleashed a reign of terror on vulnerable castes, communities and regions. Obscurantist sentiments and fundamentalist ideologies are mobilised for this purpose, the state then acquires more firepower, now legitimised in the name of threats to national and cultural unity. In the process, the social movements that had challenged the hegemony of the upper classes earlier are undermined. Draconian laws against terrorism are enacted and then used to deal with popular unrest and suppress social movements. This extremely serious development has been a direct consequence of the ruling elite wanting to somehow hang on to power and, to this end, inject the political process with strong doses of violence and civil strife. The caste and class basis of social interactions are communalised, threatening to tear the social fabric.

We are, in fact, witness to the rise of not one but two new ideologies—technologism and fundamentalism. And as the two coalesce, the exercise of power becomes increasingly cynical. The result is civil war, ethnicisation of civil society and collapse of secularism as a mode of organising plural societies. Technologism and fundamentalism undermine the very idea of pluralism and the conception of unity that not only respects diversity but also draws its resilience and strength from it. In countries like India where a large majority is able to steamroll the entire society into a monolithic whole, the majority is also found to become privy to the homogenising drive of the modern corporate capitalist state.

Rise of the Masses

Let us now turn to the masses, having considered at some length the dominant classes and the state they have come to control, camouflage and commandeer. The question is: How did the masses allow the classes and the state to stampede them into what looks like abject surrender, especially in this supposed age of the masses? In reality, there has been a flurry of mass action, in various social settings, at a variety of sites, at many levels. There has also been a spurt of state repression, usually at local and para-local levels, but also at the urban metropolitan areas, including the capitals of countries. At the same time there has been an increase in economic exploitation, not just in wage–capital relationship but also in terms of the new production relations of the corporate capitalist age. Wanton distortion of the laws and resource allocations that are still there for the poor, the backward and the destitute is also taking place.

It is against this match of opposing forces, this deadlock, this tension, this peculiar state of stagnation and exhaustion that we have to evaluate the actual condition in which the mass of people find themselves. There is, first, as already mentioned, the continuing drudgery of so-called work that must go on, for the system demands it, even under deteriorating conditions. Second, the ruling class has the capacity to divide and split the labouring classes, break their strikes and bring in outsiders to incapacitate the protesters. This follows the perception that scarcity and poverty are best conditions for demobilisation than mobilisation. In rural areas and tribal belts even this may not be necessary, for the feudal order in league with the bourgeois state ensures the full success of the exploitative chain. The rural poor survive by surrendering. Third, beyond the drudgery, divisions and the chain of exploitation, there exists the deep and pervasive conditioning of the mind of the masses by the powerful modern communication media and the deep schism and fear created by fundamentalism. The unfortunate fact is that the masses are more duped by both these latter factors than the classes, for they have little information to help them make a more discerning choice. Such all round conditioning contributes further to systemic exploitation.

And yet we know that the masses are on the move—despite the drudgery, the exploitation and the conditioning. There is a great spurt in consciousness and willingness to challenge hegemonies and unearned privileges, to protest against injustices and to mobilise horizontally to deal with oppressions. There is no doubt awareness and resistance exist and are growing. What is it then that prevents it all from crystallising into an effective counter-force against drudgery, inhuman exploitation and involuntary conditioning?

The Crux of the Problem

The masses in the postcolonial world are unorganised, they lack politicisation, they are unable to withstand cooption and conditioning despite constant struggle and growing consciousness.

The poor, the minorities, those outside the mainstream of civil society – the tribals, large segments of women – all suffer from this state of deep disorganisation. The typical avenues of mass mobilisation and redress for disabilities and deprivation – political parties and trade unions – have given way before seductive and corrupting forces. Unfortunately political parties have lost their capacity to serve the masses, particularly the destitute and the backward. As regards the trade unions, they have collapsed, no longer able to function as catalysts of a working class consciousness and a working class movement. Even the press and the judiciary are failing in their appointed tasks, they too are being corrupted by the theory of development and the miasma of a national security state backed by corrosive fundamentalism. The masses are on the rise but the institutional channels through which they ought to have found expression and which should have provided a springboard of radical action are absent, or have been simply coopted and corrupted. In this state of vacuum, within the traditional infrastructure of the liberal polity, the real new challenge of electoral politics and the multilevel politics of state and regional power are emerging. And citizens are mobilising, not in the form of typical confrontation between the so-called haves and have-nots within the conventional economic space once occupied by trade unions, nor in the equally conventional space occupied by political parties. Replacing these is the new arena of counter-action, countervailing tendencies and counter-cultural movements.

The New Challenge

It is necessary to understand the nature of this fresh challenge to existing models of thought and action. It is composed of a series of obvious and inevitable strands—struggles against existing hegemonies, organised resistance, mainstream protest, civil liberties and democratic rights. But the challenge is more basic, it is an effort to redefine the scope and range of politics. It is an effort to open up new spaces in both the arena of the state and in several other spheres of civil society outside the framework of the state. This challenge is based on new spurts in consciousness beyond economism, specific definitions of the political process, the facile and false dichotomy of state versus market, and dehumanising religiosity and modernity. It lies in discovering new indigenous roots of sustenance and strength, based not on the fractured old or the mediocre and insipid new, but on genuine possibilities of alternatives that can work. It is through generating these twin processes of conscientisation and engaging in actual struggles as well as searching for new alternatives, that there has emerged a whole new class of people known as *activists*. Drawn in the main from the conscious, enlightened and troubled streams of the middle class engaged in a wide range of activities—from sarvodaya-style units of constructive work and NGO-type development projects to more struggle-oriented political work. It is from this convergence of a conscious and restless people and a conscientious and equally restless class of volunteer politicians (to be distinguished from professional party politicians) that the new grassroots movements are taking shape. It is a convergence that enables a macro-perspective of the thousands of micro-struggles and experiments.

The scope and range of politics are being redefined with the coming together of new grassroots politics and new grassroots thinking. On the basis of these redefinitions new social movements are emerging. These movements range over a variety of issues—environment, rights of women, health, food and nutrition, education, shelter and housing, dispensation of justice, communication and dissemination of information, culture and lifestyle, and achievement of peace and disarmament. None of these were once considered suitable subject matter for politics, certainly not for mass politics in which ordinary people were involved.

Ecology can no longer be left to experts in ecological or economic development, not even to departments of environment, though the very establishment of such departments is itself a concession to popular political pressure. Nor can ecological considerations be set aside to be sorted out in the future presuming that the environmental erosion caused by development and technology in the short term can be remedied in the long term. The preservation of the environment cannot be left to the good intentions and pious declarations of governments and international agencies, but must become part of the people's own concern. This concern has spurred a variety of agitations and movements to restrain state and corporate interests from ruining the life chances of both present and future generations of all species. Concern for nature and for reversing the rapacious approach inherent in modern science and technology is becoming part of a political movement, worldwide and within individual societies.

Similarly health, food and nutrition were completely entrusted to specialists, experts and ministries peopled by them. The new hazards to health, new epidemics and horrors created by modern drugs are in good part the products of experts, doctors, and the dominant streams in the medical profession and the multibillion dollar global drug industry. Consider the availability of and access and entitlement to food, to minimum nutrition, to shelter and housing. These are among the most serious problems in distributive politics and the clearest refutation of the logic of development based on accumulation and production, with distribution to be taken care of at a later stage. Implied in that logic is the treatment of people as beneficiaries of the development process and not as direct participants in it.

Education has become an instrument of subjugation of the people instead of being the means to liberation. The lesson is the same: education cannot be left to the educationists. This perspective – of de-expertising and debureaucratising the provision of basic needs – is seeping into the grassroots political process and generating a new agenda of concerns.

New Perceptions of Reality

The faith in green and white revolutions, in the revolution in materials technology and so-called cheap-housing has been shattered with the realisation of growing hunger and malnutrition, of millions living in slums and on pavements. These are matters of empowerment and rights for which people will have to fight; not just at the level of securing more, but of devising alternatives. Even learned and technical matters such as dispensation of justice and communication of information are being subjected to public gaze and people's direct involvement. The rise of public interest litigation and the growth of investigative journalism, involving human rights activists, have together generated a strong movement for civil liberties and democratic rights.

Nowhere is the enlargement and redefinition of the scope of politics brought out as vividly and dramatically as in the women's movement. The personal and the political were considered discrete entities. A massive shift has been enacted in the understanding of women's position in politics and our conception of politics as such, with the revolutionising feminist perspective of the personal as the political and the political as the personal. In the process, new approaches and methods to deal with problems of the environment, health and sanitation are being evolved. The ecological, feminist and peace movements are converging. This has already happened in Europe with the spectacular spread of the peace movement, with the affirmation that peace and disarmament are too important to be left to governments. Women have played a major role in the movement towards these new perceptions. This is yet to happen in full measure in South

Asia, given the powerful hold of conspiracy theories of internal and external threats. But it has started happening here too; we cannot afford to remain prisoners of the arms race. Women's participation in changing this situation is growing.

As feminist values become more generalised and encompassing, a holistic approach to life will develop, which goes against the grain of modern scientific culture with its emphasis on specialisation. A holistic approach that is also pluralist and based on complementarities is more likely to happen in the non-western world than in the west.

Alternatives

Can these movements, produce a macro-challenge, a general transformation? The analysis and prognosis presented here says that this cannot be achieved through the conventional channels of political parties, trade union activity, peasant organisations and capture of state power through electoral mobilisation by political parties. We need new building blocks, to be acquired through non-party political process; through counter-cultural and alternative movements that are global in scope; and through movements for regional autonomy and a pluralist social order. The emerging counter-trends indicate a political convergence of class, culture, gender and environment. These have not yet acquired high probability but which alone can enable us to end the scenario that we are fast moving towards—of two worlds, based on a technocratic and militarised vision. This has to be in close alliance with the more economic forms of struggle for fair wages and dignity in treatment of those occupying the social peripheries.

The Growth of Non-Party Political Process

Non-party political process is not hostile to the party political process. On the contrary, it will revitalise the party political space, correct its inadequacies, and most of all provide a constant grassroots infrastructural framework to the whole political process. This process will lead to the direct involvement of people in both non-party and the party political spaces, and an organic conception of an autonomous grassroots politics will take place instead of a derivative of elite politics.

Yet it is a conception of politics different from conventional party politics, for state power is neither the only nor even the predominant object of politics. It sees an equal and perhaps even greater necessity to keep struggling against injustices which are bound to occur, no matter which party or coalition of parties is in power. Non-party political process involves experimenting with new modes of organising social, economic and technological spaces; insisting on norms in politics; and keeping the intellectual ferment alive so that state-based politics does not become an orthodoxy. It is not enough to provide participation in the system, even if this could be made less formal and more substantive. The aim is also to create a just society. Participation is necessary but not sufficient for this to happen. For that we need self-government, a decentralised order through which the masses are empowered; decentralisation not in the sense of some territorial scheme of devolution of functions and resources to lower levels, but decentralisation in which the people are the centre. It is towards this end that the various alternative social movements, alongside working class and peasant movements, have a role to play. One without the other cannot bring about the necessary transformation—a coalition of social movements and those engaged in mass struggle is absolutely necessary.

A Different Social Context

There is, moreover, a socio-demographic reason why such a direct and dynamic role of mass politics of the grassroots variety becomes necessary, quite apart from being desirable. In a predominantly rural society of great diversity, party formations like the various social democratic or labour parties that emerged in western Europe and heralded the dawn of a mass age are not likely to emerge. Without such formations and the pressure they generated in the west, the phenomenon of the modern welfare state would not have happened. So on both these counts – the role of parties and that of the state – we need to think wholly afresh, transcending all that we imported. And as we do this we will see that there is no choice but to move towards a pluralist, decentralised polity with humane technology and relatively self-reliant economy, self-reliant for the people and not just for the state. In the Indian context a just society cannot be built under the aegis of the state or through upsurges within the party systems. We just cannot afford to hand things over to bureaucrats and experts. Following the western model will create a dual society with large masses left out of citizenship, lacking basic civic rights.

Fundamentally, the vision that informs the grassroots model of mass politics, in contrast to the parliamentary or presidential model, is one in which the people are more important than the state. This point is crucial and not as simple as it sounds. In fact, in the times we are living in, it is a revolutionary idea. The dominant tendency and mode of thought today is to place the state above the people, the security of the nation state above people's security, the removal of real or imaginary threats to the state rather than dealing with persistant threats to the people and their survival. On the other hand, to restore to the people their sovereignty, will not undermine the role of the state but transform it.

Transforming the State

The transformation of the state can be achieved in four simple ways. First, the transformation is to be achieved through the transformation of civil society, not the other way round in which the state was to be the author of social transformation—a real misjudgment of the processes and pitfalls of secular power. Second, the role of the centralised state must decline. Some functions will have to be carried out by a centralised apparatus, but it is to operate in concert with other centres as well as institutional spaces in civil society. Third, the state should be enabled to regain its autonomy from dominant interests and classes; it should be gradually planned and prepared to wither away as an instrument of class and ethnic oppression and yet enabled to survive, and survive effectively, as a mediator in conflicts that will continue to take place in civil society. And fourth, we will need to move beyond the nation state syndrome which has been the source of both authoritarianism and hegemonism in our times. So long as the national security state rules the roost, the masses cannot and will not come into their own. We shall, of course, continue to need the nation state, if for nothing else, to counter the globalising and hegemonising strands in the world. And as we begin to bring it back in, we will need to once again think of the state as an instrument of freedom, equity and liberation. All that we know now is that for the state to return to such a role, it will need to relate in a continuous and organic manner with the new sources of people's empowerment—from the institutional spaces involved in the non-party political process, to the spaces that have mushroomed in the arena of grassroots politics through the growing role of activists-cum-intellectuals, to the arena of people's movements in which dalits, adivasis, women and other oppressed are getting engaged. Only so shall we rein in the state to be part of the alternative movements, and in the process transform it.

5

Democracy and the Role of the State

We have considered the broad historical context of the changing role of the state, from centrality to gradual sidelining, to reassertion through the transformation of its role. We now need to address a basic issue with regard to democracy—how the very process of building a democratic polity makes the transformation of the nation state necessary, in order to provide a relevant institutional framework for such a polity. Undertaking such a task in a country like India where a massive erosion of the institutions of the state has already happened, is a great challenge. Independent India began with a model of nation building in which the state retained a large measure of autonomy, intervened in the socioeconomic spheres with its own agenda of social change, and was relatively free of vested interests that operated in the economic sphere and the social arena where class, caste and communal interests prevailed. Such freedom from entrenched interests ensured the autonomy of the political process. In course of time the state even became the prime mover of initiatives with the ability to set priorities in the social arena. The state was able to permeate different segments and levels of social reality. If some areas were left uncovered, it was because commitment to a democratic ideology and pluralist society did not permit straitjacketing of the social order. At local and regional levels political leaders may have often found it expedient to operate through entrenched elites and available social structures. But neither of these prevented the nation state from pursuing its own policies and priorities.

During the 1950s, 60s and early 70s, politics was not an epiphenomenon. The state was not just an agent of the ruling class. In fact, there was no homogeneous ruling class—a term that makes more sense today than it did then. The ruling class was not the prime mover but the state. The bourgeoisie and the landed gentry were weak and fragmented compared to the power and authority of the state. The state was seen by the people as an instrument for countering the more serious reflections of social inequality.

The state's autonomy from dominant interests and its capacity to promote the larger social good has deteriorated. The undermining of the party system, the federal polity and the intermediate structures through which local problems and conflicts were resolved has deprived the state's capacity for enabling social transformation and has, instead, made it vulnerable to dominant interests. Ironically, greater centralisation of power has made the state less autonomous; whereas distancing itself from lower tiers of the federal structure, and from party and bureaucratic institutions, has made it dependent on dominant structures of national and international power and privilege.

It is important to gauge the nature of the shift in thinking, among the elite in India, on the role of the state. For long there was belief in the positive role of the state in both setting up the 'commanding heights' of the economy and achieving a measure of self-reliance through import substitution, as the local bourgeoisie was considered too weak to undertake these tasks. The same bourgeoisie was able to expand its base and gain access to large-scale financial resources mobilised by the state apparatuses as a result of the state's institutional expansion and new ideological thrusts.

Indeed, the state's role benefited the capitalist class. While the state retained the capacity to formulate an overall framework of policies and priorities, the private sector found it expedient to accept this. This was the era of mixed economy in which state capitalism, rather than the socialist state, played a catalytic role. But even this began to change after the mid 1970s. Once their consumer needs were gratified with the construction of an industrial infrastructure, the elite classes had no use for state interventions in the economy. It was between 1967 and 1977 that the aspirations of the masses began to rise, and the state was asked to take on the task of increasing the purchasing power of the people with redistributive measures.

It is this change in the perception of the elite classes that spurred transnational agencies like the IMF and the World Bank to come forward with a package of liberalisation, export orientation and technology transfer. The last allowed for collaboration with multinationals for modernising the economy and enmeshing it into the global market. This convergence – of the shift in local industrial capital and the national elite's thinking on the role of the state; the growing availability of international capital for India, promoted mainly by the World Bank; and the will to withstand pressures for distributive justice within the country – set the stage for the Indian state to be conceived, for the first time, as an agent and collaborator of world capitalism. Not only did the state lose its autonomy from dominant interests, it was actually found willing to relinquish its erstwhile role of ushering basic social reforms. Meanwhile, the political terrain came under the sway of communal and religious appeals, relegating the concern for social justice and people's survival to the background.

The decline in the autonomy of the state has been accompanied by its growing delegitimisation. The new elite condemns the state making use of criticisms emanating from both the left and the right. The instruments of the state – government, bureaucracy, judiciary, parliament and political parties – are no longer considered efficient means for progress and for the march into the new millennium. They are perceived as impediments, necessary perhaps for maintaining a democratic facade, but peripheral to the more dynamic thrust of modern technology and management. Factors responsible for the massive shift in perception of the market, rather than the state, as the agent of national development are—the process of debureaucratising the state apparatus; the switch from the public to the private sector; and the growing importance of autonomous corporations in dairy, forestry, biotechnology, atomic energy and telecommunications that are accountable neither to parliament nor to the ministries. The marginalisation of the masses, the destitution of the poor and the exploitation of natural resources for private industrial needs are accepted as necessary costs that the nation must pay for progress, for achieving national power, and for attempting to catch up with the developed countries.

These developments are sought to be kept away from the public gaze by filtering media coverage. Focus on the state and public policy kept the focus on poverty and the people alive. With the state and its agencies downgraded, the problem of poverty too is abandoned. Therefore the role of the state as an agent of democratic transformation has also deteriorated.

Debureaucratisation

The smartest move in debureaucratisation has been in an area that would be least suspected of being subject to manipulation—the government's announcement to involve the voluntary sector, i.e. the NGOs, in development. The seventh plan document devoted a whole chapter to this approach. On the face of it, nothing could be more liberalising—indeed, liberating. It would end dependence on foreign funds, enable voluntary bodies to come together on a common platform irrespective of ideological and other differences, and equip themselves to assume a major role in development. They would even in be able to reach out to the people, which the government has been unable to do.

The enthusiasm for voluntary organisations has been part of a major ideological shift, emanating from the World Bank and its global corporate allies. According to this thinking, a freshly conceived private sector, including the NGOs, provides a new frontier for a dynamic technological drive. This perspective is shared by important world institutions involved in development —the World Bank, the IMF, the World Trade Organization (WTO), and also the United Nations Development Programme (UNDP), the single largest agency for channelling international funding to governments and individual ministries. Various other donor agencies are also discovering in the NGO model an effective instrument for penetrating rural economies, forests and alternative energy sources.

This penetration is to be achieved through a wide diffusion of liberalised, privatised efforts. Vast hinterlands are to be opened up, new technologies introduced and a high rate of economic surplus generated for the metropolitan regions and the export market. All this is to be done cost effectively through cheap labour and raw materials, and in the framework of competitive ethos which the market provides and the state cannot.

The rapacious drive of a transnationalised, technology-driven capitalism and the realisation that earlier avenues of investment in urban-based industries were drying up or getting too competitive, lie behind the new thinking. The state and its agencies were suitable for the earlier model of building an economy of commanding heights. They were in fact better than the private sector, as the required investment in massive infrastructures could only be provided by the state. But the agencies of the state are insufficient for the new model of capitalism.

A democratically elected government that pursues policies that adversely affect the poor is forced to engage in doublespeak. This is not always evident. In India, for instance, we know that landed interests oppress and exploit the landless, and visit them with atrocities at the hint of resistance. We know that the urban rich are getting richer by encroaching and appropriating land and other means of livelihood of the rural poor. We know that there is growing greed and hunger for agricultural land and that hundreds of thousands of villagers and tribals are being deprived of their land and forced to migrate. But we hesitate to think that the governments, presumably representing national interest, are privy to the exploiters—the landowners, the moneylenders, the capitalist class and the foreign elements. We prefer not to acknowledge the existence of an intimate relationship between the exploiters and the governments we have elected.

Governments world over are becoming more and more opaque, with their inner workings not transparent to the public. They advance the plea of public interest to keep the public uninformed or even misinformed. Documents are marked 'confidential' and 'secret' and even elected members of parliament are bluntly refused information. Under the circumstances it is difficult to acquire knowledge of decisions and decision-makers. Speculation and rumours are rife and the mass media has ceased to keep the public informed.

More subtle is the information overflow through the media, through policy pronouncements providing declarations of principled and bold commitments by senior leaders, through slogans and metaphors that have a populist ring. Big business is denounced, poverty alleviation is accorded high priority and large schemes for meeting the basic needs of the people are launched. Publicity campaigns are mounted to protect the environment, clean up rivers and replant forests on a massive scale, utilising the latest technology, imploring people to cooperate. As the traditional agencies of the state and bureaucracy are held responsible for depriving people of access to natural resources, autonomous agencies and corporations are entrusted with these tasks; voluntary bodies and people's organisations are also sought for these tasks.

It appears as if we are entering a whole new world—new thinking; a new generation of not just leaders but ideas; a new structure of governance run not by discredited politicians and corrupt bureaucrats but by a committed band of professionals, who are also presumably in touch with the latest in science and technology.

This apparently fresh and innovative approach has also adopted the jargon of the anti-establishment critics of the state. A corporate rather than bureaucratic structure makes it possible to create entities that are not accountable to the normal machinery of constitutional government and parliament. The overtures and offers of largesse to voluntary agencies and people's organisations make it possible to coopt sources of dissent. The claim of greater professionalism is suspect, because the real experts in specific fields – ecology, water resources, or health and nutrition – have been replaced by managers, advertisers, foreign-foundation personnel and well-connected journalists who are adept at hijacking the work of genuine professionals. Together, these forays into governing structures have undermined accountability to elected representatives, and enabled industrial houses and the transnationals, hitherto suspect in India, to find direct entry into the system.

The Rise of a New Vision

We may well be stepping into an age which will make us a highly vulnerable society and polity, largely due to the new vision taking hold of elites. India's earlier resistance to global fashions, and proverbial resilience and insularity may well crumble before this vision. It is the vision of a technologically advanced society providing new opportunities and possibilities. We were attracted by concepts like development and modernisation earlier, but we fashioned them to suit our preferred ideals of national self-reliance and cultural autonomy. The vision that is now taking hold of Indians is of an altogether different variety. It is a vision that has already derailed many other societies, their cultures, their ideological balance, their very patterns of livelihood and existence.

The crux of the new vision is provided by the new technologies—the information and communication technologies based on the microelectronics revolution found in the operations of banks, airlines and of parliament. The masses do not have much use for these technologies. But then neither do these directly threaten their survival. They will lose in the long run, as the mass media homogenise their lifestyles and cultures. Meanwhile, the corporate sector will gain immensely from privatisation of telecommunications, subsidised facilities for business houses and collaborations with multinationals. For, the direction of microelectronics is being dictated by corporate demands, not social needs, despite protests from patriotic Indian experts.

It is the second group of the new technologies – biotechnologies – that will threaten the resource base and survival prospects of the poor. Insidious in nature, they are more dangerous than the nuclear threat, for engineered life forms are largely invisible and their impact on human, plant and animal life completely unknown. Nuclear plants and explosions can be seen and heard. Microorganisms are invisible and their effect irreversible. Nuclear radiation cannot multiply, but living organisms can. Qualities of invisibility and speedy reproduction could cause an ecological holocaust that has been imagined and simulated only in defense and corporate labs. Biotechnology provides fresh opportunities for the corporate sector at a time of shrinking opportunities caused by the failure of the green revolution. Biotechnology also constitutes a threat because it allows the intensification of the use of pesticides and herbicides.

The mystification engendered by the label 'new technologies' disguises the decline of access and the narrowing down of entitlements through the sheer robbery of land and genetic resources. Ultimately, biotechnology is an efficient means for transnational corporations to convert genetic resources accessible to people into commodities that these corporations will sell. As the corporations turn resources into sources of profit, resources become less and less available to people as sources of sustenance. The dawn of the twenty-first century has already witnessed the erosion of the livelihoods of people through displacement. Breeding tomatoes that will be processed for export is not meant to solve the problem of the hunger of marginalised Indians. On the contrary, by taking land and genetic resources away from the poor, biotechnology aggravates the problem of hunger. The prospects offered by new technologies for the masses and for the big businesses are different. The 'new millennium' for the poor will thus be very different from the new millennium for the rich.

The Changing Nature of Capitalism

Underlying the new technological paradigm and vision is the striking change that has taken place in the nature of international capitalism and the world economy. It is no longer necessary to have captive markets for the supply of consumer or even capital goods produced in the North. Now former colonies produce these goods with dechining profit margins, while their costs in pollution and labour management are steadily rising. Control is exercised with regard to critical research and development on intellectual properties like patents and basic know-how that is stowed away in coded secrecy. For example, the minutiae of location and spread of natural resources; the centralised storage of diverse properties like seeds and catchments through networks of hired scientists engaged in economic espionage; new modules of satellite surveillance; and crucial components of the new technological landscape like the computer chip. The capacity to render technological packages obsolete has also grown. Therefore those keen on the latest in technology are assigned the status of being perennially dependent. We know this to be the case in both military and civilian technologies, reflected in the ever-growing deficit balance of payments and indebtedness of third world countries. The NICs of Latin America and Southeast Asia have already been victimised. Countries like China and India have the potential to be even more dependent. They have been successfully sold the highly seductive label of becoming the new industrial giants of the world, and the tantalising prospect of becoming regional superpowers.

The ideas of world capitalism based on colonial-style economics providing captive markets and exploitation of labour, and of world imperialism based on a number of weak dependencies, have already become outdated. The new thinking, and language, of managing the world is that of a world order based on the interdependence between the established major powers wielding extraordinary technological and financial resources (the United States, Japan, the European Economic Community) and a select set of client states (Russia, China, India).

Together, these have the potential to create one integrated global order – of techno-economic, strategic and military power – from which a large number of nation states and their enormous populations are marginalised, excluded and considered dispensable, as historically superfluous and anachronistic. In this integrated world order of cooperating states, all possible conflicts of interest and ideological struggles are to be negotiated and ultimately eschewed. This order assumes precedence over sovereign nation states representing specific populations. Disarmament between major powers could be followed by high growth industrialisation, leaving out concerns like class conflict, historical antagonisms and cultural plurality.

The corporate mind-set informing the concept of the world order is not unfamiliar. What is new is that the leaders of erstwhile sources of challenge to western hegemony are becoming pliant and readily available converts to the world order. At every stage in the unfolding of this world order there is doublespeak—on ecology, integrity of cultures, increasing communications, intellectual freedom, human rights and economic development.

The New Dominion

We can now bring together the various threads of our empirical analysis and return to the theoretical issue posed at the beginning: how, over time, the nation states that came into being after the Second World War and began asserting their autonomy and sovereignty have been brought back into the fold of the global capitalist order. In order to understand this turnaround, we need to see how colonial-type bondage was substituted by greater and stronger integration into both the global capitalist market and the strategic straitjacket fashioned by leading arms producers. Our existing conceptual categories of historical analysis are ill-equipped to grasp the full implications of this split in the human community occasioned precisely by its greater integration, globalisation and homogenisation. As mentioned in Chapter 4, most existing ideologies and their conceptual offshoots grew in the typical European setting of nation states, during the process of first-generation industrialisation and against the background of essentially class-based identities. These ideologies seem insufficient to deal with a transnationalised world in which the dominant currency is technology.

This insufficiency is also reflected at the level of organisation of productive forces. Today, we are confronted with a completely different model of world capitalism, a switch from the European to the American model. Technology as a system is propelled by communication and information orders conditioning human minds, and by corporate forms of organisation conditioning the behaviour of states. All other relations of production are made subordinate to technology. This has generally forced all other systems – socialist, third world, Japanese – to accede and measure success in terms laid down by the American cultural syndrome.

Ecological Erosion

The domination of technology and its pervasive impact on politics, economics and security, has in turn caused a massive erosion of the ecological basis of human civilisation. It has destroyed the resource base of the people, especially the millions of rural, tribal and ethnic poor whose populations are dispensable in the aggressive march of high-tech capitalism. Their traditional access to natural resources and non-commercial products has been blocked. The situation common amongst even the most remote hill peoples: the military builds roads, urban and tourist traffic moves in with artifacts and consumer goods, modern communications hard sell these products, and modern technology crowns these activities with a series of bilateral and multilateral deals. The bounties of nature that were traditionally freely available to these peoples are bled dry.

The Future of the State as an Institution

We can draw together our analysis of the multiple dimensions of the historical epoch in which we find ourselves by focussing on the central issue of our times: the changing nature of the state and its role in civil society, especially as it impinges on the people of the third world. We need to reexamine our assumptions about the state's presumed role as the liberator, equaliser, moderniser and mobiliser.

The state and its relationship to the people is the relationship and between the principal carrier of modern capitalism and technology, and the social order. Here, a major part of the social order is marginalised. For example, between the military and the civil order; between the development policies of the state and its transnational sponsors, and the economic and ecological catastrophes affecting the masses; between the global information order and the citizen reduced to a package of consumption; and between dominant races and power structures controlling the state, and those at the periphery, presumably still members of the civil order but progressively being pushed out by repressive and genocidal politics, the former elements appear to be gaining ground. It is this capture of the state by a convergence of class, ethnic, technological and military actors, developmentalists, communicators and managers, including managers of votes, that has set the stage for the present confrontation between the classes and the masses.

The presumptions that once existed – of the state being relatively autonomous of entrenched interests and classes; of the state being an independent actor with the power to influence, discipline and even coerce established interests to accept policies aimed at transforming the status quo – are being severely questioned.

The expectation of such a role for the state, and of the presumed alliance between the state and the masses, has been belied. Today the state is seen to have betrayed the masses. It has failed to provide the means for a radical bourgeois transformation from which a revolutionary alternative could emerge. The state has degenerated into a technocratic machine serving a small group that is kept in power by heavy security at the top and a regime of repression and terror at the bottom.

Undermining of the Political Process and its Impact

The change in the nature of the state is fast undermining the factors that had prevented the state from becoming too centralised and antithetical to the interests of the people, and had preserved the autonomy of the state vis-à-vis dominant interests and classes. In India, the state that came into being after independence had been conceived as a public arena, as a legally constituted structure of institutions that was publicly accountable and functioned under public gaze. The state was not meant to be just a reflection of some dominant force, but rather it was an entity that enjoyed legitimacy and authority by virtue of widespread consensus.

Even if the deprived sections of the people and various peripheral communities did not enjoy access to the state as did the more privileged and upwardly mobile strata, it was still not a closed shop or a private domain. In fact, the opportunities for access and participation were supposed to expand—an idea in which the masses believed for a fairly long period of time. It was through the mechanisms of the state that the deprived and excluded strata perceived the possibility of their inclusion. This had to happen politically as there was little scope for them outside the political arena of the state. They had rights vis-à-vis the state, and none outside of it (except perhaps in their own communities). They had no option but to participate in the political process and, through that, press their claims on the state. This accounts for the long-held view of the Indian state as democratic and possessing socialist ideological leanings.

Three crucial elements had contributed to such an ideological predisposition. First, that democratic politics was to be the main instrument of social transformation. Second, that it was to operate through institutions that were conceived as public in nature and hence accountable to the people. And third, that the state was to occupy a central role in this process of transformation, not by aligning with private interests but by being autonomous of those interests. Some may even argue that private interests did not seek to permeate the political process. But if they did try, they needed to prevented. And to the extent lags occurred, the democratic process would fill up such lags.

Now both beliefs – of the autonomy of the Indian state and its accountability through democratic functioning – are no longer valid. Democratic institutions, the rule of law, and the accountability of the government and other institutions of the state have been eroded. The erosion happened over a long period of time—the weakening of the party system and parliamentary and federal institutions under Indira Gandhi; the rise of political corruption that began with direct mobilisation of funds through systematic cuts and kickbacks that began under Sanjay Gandhi and has multiplied since; and the increasingly centralised and arbitrary use of the public domain resulting from the decline of the political process initiated during the Emergency.

And yet, with all this, the state still has retained its character as a public arena and has continued to insist on its relative autonomy, particularly in regard to external interests. It has become vulnerable because of its weakening as a democratic arena. It is the shift in basic ideology that has caused the turnaround, making it a captive of transnational capitalism and private internal forces in league with transnational interests. It is the ideology of privatisation that is sweeping across the world and is taking hold of, and being utilised by, politicians and bureaucrats in the third world. The bureaucrats have lost confidence in their earlier vision and perspective and have been looking for a magic wand that would enable them to clear up the political mess they had gotten into.

Conclusion

It is the power of this new thinking – which at once compromises the autonomy and integrity of the nation state and undermines the democratic character of the political process, marginalising and excluding large sections of society from the state's purview – that makes for effective control of the state by local and global corporate capitalist interests. This was not so during the Indian national movement for independence or in the decades that followed when commercial interests were seeking to influence the running of the state.

This chapter has attempted to examine the relationship between capitalism and the state with reference to the complex historical forces that have been at work, rather than to any preconceived theory about the state being a prisoner of the ruling class. It is only by examination can we get a full measure of the manner in which both the state and the political process have come under the dominion of world capitalism and how, in turn, this has consolidated authoritarian and centralising tendencies.

The rise of a technocratic mode of capitalism is responsible for the existing state of affairs. This mode of capitalism is transnational and universal in character. It is the sweep of this historical process that has helped promote the corporate capitalist model over the nation state in the third world and the former socialist world. Until we realise and acknowledge the fundamentally changed nature of capitalism from the time of the first industrial revolution, we will not be able to grasp the broad historical process.

6

Rebuilding the State

The Indian state has been affected by other forces at work, apart from the latest phase of capitalism. Most of these forces are indigenous and located within the framework of the modern state. The years since the Emergency have exposed our collective inadequacies, and have led to the realisation that something different is required rather than the repetition of the institutional framework provided by the Westminster model, or changing ruling groups at the top and middle tiers. Those who had for so long pinned hope on any specific party, group or individual for showing a way out have been disappointed. There are no easy solutions to a situation caused by the continuing erosion of a system. But if the erosion is allowed to continue, it could well lead to a breakdown.

From the 1980s crime and violence have been on the upswing. The lower classes and the vulnerable strata of society – women, poorer strata of dalits and Muslims, those engaged in exposing societal malaise and therefore drawn towards militancy – have suffered severely, sometimes even physical dismemberment and death. Individual safety and security have declined precipitously. *Goonda raj* is on the rise and is often promoted by the strong men of politics. Communities have been attacked in the presence of police. There is a growing feeling among sections of the people that one has to fend for oneself by any means possible.

Meanwhile, there are signs of disquiet brewing in the ranks of the police and other security forces, and resentment at the frequent recourse to calling in the army in situations that should have been handled by the regular mechanisms of order and security. Parliamentary politics have failed to reflect public opinion or decisively respond to conditions of growing agony and alienation. Political parties have long ceased to mediate in conflict situations, containing them locally and preventing their spread. Communal riots and other forms of violence now spread from one area (or community) to another. These riots can go on for months, as it happened in shocking and traumatic ways in Gujarat during 2002.

The centre has proved incapable of dealing with the deep fissures in the border states and major challenges in other states. The federal structure is under severe strain with party politics of the mafia variety getting the better of governmental process. The top and middle echelons of the bureaucracy and intelligence agencies feel powerless with regard to mafia politicians. The economy is in disarray. Restlessness and disorder are once again raising their heads in the campuses, and the youth of the country feels alienated.

Instead of responding to these and many other manifestations of the breakdown of the system there has been glib talk from the ruling circles of growing dangers from abroad against which the nation must be prepared. From the opposition there has been equally glib talk of the imminent fall of the government, each time hoping to force a mid-term election on the country. The political elite – ruling and oppositional – seem to have lost all sense of proportion.

Large-scale violation of basic norms for personal gain has already taken place. Accumulation of evidence (involving not just members from the dominant ruling elite but also a number of other highly placed leaders) over the years and has sharply brought down the credibility of politicians. The manner in which party and electoral funds have been collected, has led to a consolidation of entrenched interests and the growing exploitation of the doctrines of the state for private ends. It appears as if the state has become a source of munificence and plunder. The decade from the mid 1970s to the mid 1980s saw corruption being systematised through close linkage between financial, bureaucratic and political groupings within the confines of the state. And with the 1990s came the dominion of the market against the state.

The transformation in the nature of the state can be traced back to the perpetuation of poverty and deprivation, of shortages and inflation, and of a thriving parallel economy. If the present nexus between economic interests and the political and bureaucratic elite is allowed to continue, it will not be long before the state is trapped in a virtual siege by a small coterie. This has already happened in a number of other third world societies and India too seems to be moving towards such a state of affairs. The only difference has been that, due to the massive politicisation of the lower classes and the deprived strata of society, a conflict is raging against those who would profit from such a structure of economic and political patronage. All of which is leading to rising unrest, violence, insecurity and uncertainty, and to the unsettling of institutional relations and the blockage of communication channels, promoted by sections of the ruling class. There is also the growing isolation of various social strata and regions, engendering the erosion and ultimate collapse of the state on which the poor and the deprived are dependent.

Decline of the State

The state in India faces a most complex situation that has to be grasped in its totality. It is not sufficient to recognise that the democratic order is under strain or to confine attention to the threats to our liberties as citizens. The erosion of democratic institutions and values must no doubt receive urgent attention, but it is necessary to think of it as part of a much larger process of erosion and alienation. The integrity and viability of the Indian nation state – a state which had always been unstable and whose existence was contingent upon a set of shared understandings in its relationship with civil society, but which has of late been subjected to new frustrations and threats – is at stake.

The state in India, with a clear and visible centre, is relatively recent in origin. Traditionally, Indian society has been largely apolitical—in the sense that its antecedent networks and institutions had little experience of secular authority of the modern type, and that it had also lacked a clear centre. For short periods of time, when a single centre did emerge (say in the form of a specific dynasty assuming widespread power), it was based more on relative power compared to other centres, than on unchallenged authority. Such a society produced a collective orientation that was largely apolitical, and a view of morality with primary reference to the individual, with accent on one's own salvation. By and large there was weak institutionalisation of objective checks against misuse of power.

The British colonial impact, both territorial as well as institutional – more deeply the Congress movement for independence; and especially Gandhi's genius at channelling the collective orientations and strains of self-transcendence towards a national crystallisation – laid the basis of the new Indian state. Cultural identities and moral dispositions were reoriented and reordered towards the Indian state. When ultimately a political system was established at the national level, it assumed the characteristic of a new all-India cultural tradition (rather than a mere juxtaposition of pre-existing communal, tribal and territorial loyalties as had happened in some colonial societies) with considerable autonomy and initiative in the hands of a new and distinctive elite.

The authority of the new elite was legitimised through a framework in which the people were made to feel they had a stake in the functioning of the new state's institutions. It was this institutional framework that enabled the dominant social strata to simultaneously engage in the accommodation of prevailing diversity and the establishment of the new elite's dominance. Combining traditional brahminic and modern secular images, this elite constituted the new priesthood of India— because of its revolutionary role in bringing about major changes; because of the exemplary life and moral stature of individuals like Gandhi; and because of the overriding importance of the politician in social life, as mediator and arbitrator in local conflicts.

There were two other reasons for the growing legitimacy of the new political elite. First, India's great political mobilisers did not view their task as hostile to local traditions in the name an unifying ideology. In fact, by drawing on the institutional structures of party and constructive work, and later on government and economic activities, and the dynamics of the village society, they established alignments with intermediate and local elites and their networks. Second, the new elite projected a vision of democratic social reconstruction which held the promise of undoing the injustices and exploitation of the pre-existing social order, and to that extent appealed not only to the masses but also to many other strata located at intermediate levels in the social hierarchy.

The accommodative and reconstructive aspects, together with the moral impact of an elite committed to the new doctrine of *sevadharma*, provided a powerful cultural thrust legitimising the new institutional order. It was on these new cultural bases that the foundations of a modern state with a clear and authoritative centre were laid. The authority of this centre rested on a corpus of institutions, operating at a number of levels and in several sectors, and involving many layers of identity – ranging from the family to the state – integrated through an active and identifiable political process.

This political process has now been eroded, and with it the institutional corpus and the psychological élan that provided the sinews of the Indian state have been weakened. Today we have a central authority without a corpus to realise its authority, a state wielding wide-ranging power without the means to exercise it, and an administrative set-up and a law-and-order machinery without a functioning hierarchy. Objectionable measures such as the Maintenance of Internal Security Act (MISA), the National Security Act (NSA), or the Prevention of Terrorism Act (POTA) would be unnecessary if institutional structures functioned properly. It is not just the democratic framework, and the much-cherished liberties and freedoms, but the very process that helps the Indian state function that is near collapse. The crisis that we face today is the crisis of the Indian state and with it of the Indian nation.

Democracy: The Larger Context

The prospects of democracy have to be seen in this larger context of creating a viable state with a recognisable and operating constitution. In a vast, socially heterogeneous and multilayered society, a state can be built and made viable only through a harmonious blending and sustained interplay of its multiplicity. Unity can only be achieved by anchoring such a society in its diversity and mobilising this diversity through a new cultural thrust. This thrust should be operationalised through a set of institutions, codes of conduct and norms of interaction that are widely accepted. And the society's elite should continuously mediate in ordering the changing equations that arise from these interactions, leading to conditions of social transformation which essentially take place at the lower level of the polity. The democratic political process in such a society must of necessity operate at many levels in the territorial and political spaces, and through a variety of organisations in the socioeconomic terrain— involving and enabling decisions that are based on certain norms of propriety and justice.

The institutional framework of democracy suffers erosion when the political process that connects the various levels and enables socioeconomic changes at the grassroots level deteriorates. And when the institutional framework weakens, the state weakens too, losing its strength and stability, sensitivity and flexibility. The diffusion happens notwithstanding the shrill noises made by politicians and the various ordinances they promulgate, through which they intend to build a strong state. These noises and the brutalities committed by the minions of the system only signal a non-existing power structure and an already enfeebled authority. This breakdown of authority and the institutions that sustain it provides the key to the crisis of the Indian state. It is the role of the state to provide conditions of security and predictability within which something as delicate as a democratic structure can operate. When the state becomes weak it is simply not possible to sustain democratic institutions and rights. The converse is also true: it is not possible to build a modern state in a country and civil society like that of India except through institutionalising a far-flung and multitiered political process involving diverse strata and sectors of society. The Indian democracy should not just mean a system of periodic elections.

It is necessary to delineate the structural and cultural implications of this argument. The usual dichotomies drawn between centralisation and decentralisation, and secular and parochial identities, are uncalled for in the Indian situation. For, these polar opposites need to be organically integrated and ordered through a given system. A strong centre cannot be built except by drawing upon the vast resources and diverse skills of the people, through a multitiered and multisectoral corpus of institutions. A centre that stands aloof and unincorporated becomes alien, loses touch, and fails to command allegiance and loyalty.

On the other hand, a decentralised institutional model cannot function effectively or prevent itself from being captured by narrow vested interests except by being organically tied to a functioning national framework of institutional linkages and policy initiatives. This necessitates a viable state apparatus and a stable centre; in the absence of such anchorage, decentralisation could well lead to fragmentation, promiscuous power games and violent social collisions that discredit the whole political process.

Similarly, for the state to acquire secular authority over a large and diverse terrain of caste and community orientations, it is necessary for it not to suppress their interplay but to order it through the political process described above. Any attempt at forced modernisation of an apolitical variety, by the centre of the system, only leads to stronger parochial reactions. On the other hand, a sustained process of politicisation serves to both underplay and reorient traditional institutions like the caste system by generating pressures for social and economic change, as well as new psychological orientations.

But once the larger institutional framework within which the process of politicisation and social change is pursued begins to get eroded, parochial identities emerge once again and assume exclusive and defiant postures. In India, now, caste and communal groupings are assuming aggressive postures, and collisions between communities have acquired communal overtones, with local party leaders and mafia elements taking advantage of it all. Therefore the electoral process gets distorted, the fear of losing votes of this or that community leads to irrational postures and deeply affects the public domain.

The erosion of institutionalised politics produces powerful parochial urges not just at the lower levels of the system or in tradition-bound segments thereof, but also within the highly secular and modern sectors and among the most highly placed. The decline of institutions is sought to be compensated by falling back on family and kin-group resources. From there it is a short step before the state is transformed into an instrument for private and parochial gains. When political power is dispensed through personalised networks and is not subjected to institutional checks, muscle power, money and mafia-style management become political currencies. This free-for-all politics flourishes under the facade of a centralised, secular and modern system presided over by 'charismatic' leaders.

Parochialism and the tendency to fragmentation are endemic to Indian reality. But when the national political centre itself becomes subject to parochial pressures the tendency is to negotiate matters of state with local potentates instead of a national elite and the state's institutional framework that is answerable to public opinion and sensitive to communication channels. The conclusion is clear: the more centralised and distant a political centre, the more the chance of its becoming personalised and parochialised, with more scope for vested interests to manipulate the state apparatus. The centre becomes weaker in relation to these interests.

The Westminster Model

If we agree that the crisis India faces arises not just from an erosion of the democratic political process but from a virtual breakdown of the state, and that the two are closely connected, then we need to pursue two goals simultaneously in building an alternative system—to build a viable state structure, and to ground such a structure in a political process that operates at multiple levels. It should be a process that fulfills two aims:

(a) enable the people of this country to take the decisions that affect their lives, and (b) create an elite that mediates and resolves the conflicts that are inherent in transformative politics. Institution building for the creation of a viable state and a functioning democracy involves both these dimensions. It involves people's participation in decision-making and the growth of an elite which not only operates through institutions that make people's participation possible at a variety of levels and in diverse settings, but also integrates it all into a common and collective endeavour. These two are also linked inextricably.

Mass awakening and pervasive politicisation can lead either to creative and revolutionary restructuring of a social order, or to chaos and breakdown under unmanageable pressures. As chaos is hardly propitious for democratic struggles against inequity and injustice, it can only lead to further repression and violence. Those who subscribe to the view that revolutions emerge only from total breakdown and chaos are indulging in irresponsible thinking.

The nature and institutional thrust of the democratic process are crucial influences in the rebuilding of the Indian state. The representative system of parliamentary democracy tends to focus on working out power equations at the top and is prone to producing large gaps in communication, affiliation and identity formation in a country that is vast, populous, socially heterogeneous and conflict ridden.

While the federal and local structures and the intra-party democracy through which the Congress system operated lasted, the centralising characteristics of the Westminster model were held in check by a multitier elite operating a multitier institutional order. When such a system gave way under the impact of populist and personalised system of governance and decision making, no effort was made to utilise populist appeal for involving the people and build an alternative institutional apparatus on that basis.

The result has been a growing hiatus between various levels and sectors of the system. It has undermined institutionalised channels of information from the middle- and the ground-level bases of the polity where massive changes were happening. It has corroded the faith of the aggrieved strata in the parliamentary framework and spurred them to resort to agitations. These agitations could not be contained at the local levels. The centre itself has not been able to cope, except through ordinances and the despatch of the Central Preserve Police Force (CRPF), the Border Security Force (BSF) and army contingents. In just a few years time, it has led to the fragmentation of the political structure and a steep decline in the performance of the system, making it insensitive to the needs and demands of the poor and the weak.

The attempt to create a centralised system thus proved abortive—centralisation without an institutionalised corpus through which the centre could operate and establish its writ and authority. Lacking a corpus, the centre became vulnerable to the pressures of entrenched interests, and forsook the allegiance of those at the regional and lower level. Once this happened to the governing centre, parliamentary and electoral institutions too proved vulnerable to the same pressures, losing their earlier influence and autonomy. These institutions became an arena for futile confrontations and hoarse invectives, with little relevance to the ground forces that were getting released. The opposition (including the left parties) gradually withdrew from the task of institutionalising their appeal and their power base at the grassroots and became embroiled in toppling the government through legislative maneuvers and electoral games.

Left to itself, the Westminster model is bound to produce such a result, for it is basically a reductionist model in which the party in power – the parliamentary party – derives its authority from the people, in turn legitimising the authority of a cabinet of ministers so long as it commands a majority of seats. The cabinet defers to the prime minister whereas the individual ministers tend to exercise their power through the regular bureaucracy. The result is a prime ministerial instead of a parliamentary system of government, the rise of an administrative state, preoccupation with holding legislative majorities and a style of mass politics that is essentially aimed at winning elections.

As electioneering becomes increasingly expensive and tortuous in the absence of an open and fully operating party structure, there takes place a significant growth in the role of money, secrecy about the sources of money and the role of professionals who can manage both grow in importance. The power to provide the money passes into the hands of the executive branch (quite often an individual entrusted with a treasurer-like role) which alone can work out the necessary quid pro quo between state patronage and political financing, including many secret and devious deals. All of this contributes to the rise of a hegemonical state controlled by a small class of professionals, a sharp decline in the power of representative bodies and the people who elect them.

The Westminster model should never be left unattended. During the 1950s and 60s it was kept in check by a series of factors: (a) the Congress system and its internal thermostat; (b) the federal political order; (c) a large infrastructure of local institutions; and (d) the growth in the importance of the voluntary sector. In states where there was a successful implementation of policies and programmes at the grassroots, there was also another major factor which incidentally is a necessary prerequisite of the democratic process: (e) political organisation of the poor and weaker sections.

Thus there existed during that period a balance between the centralising and technocratic aspects of the Westminster model, and the participatory and politicised aspects of the party system and local institutions. This balance also provided a continuum to the state through the availability and functioning of a vertical as well as horizontal institutional corpus. It is the growing imbalance of this structure in recent years that has produced an institutional as well as a power vacuum over which the supposedly strong centre is delicately perched, despite massive majorities.

The result is instability in office, a government that is constantly firefighting and therefore unable to attend to the problems of the people, and a set of mid-term elections that are fought on the single issue of who is to be put in power or brought down from power. Election after election, voters have provided massive support to the government they chose but they have no means of ensuring that the chosen government would deliver.

The political organisation of the poor and weak sections is crucial to the viability and legitimacy of the Indian state. In areas where the poor and exploited sections have been politically organised – Kerala under the first communist government and Karnataka under Devraj Urs, for example – the Westminster model was modified, or further institutionalised so that it provides a framework for channelising social conflicts and enabling submerged groups to join the battle of politics.

It is important to remember that for a long time the British model of parliamentary politics was a model of elite turnover, fashioned under conditions of a limited role for the state and before the advent of mass politics. It was the politics of well-bred gentlemen debating fine points of political theory and practice. In India too, the system worked rather well while the political process was essentially confined to the middle class with a sprinkling of a few educated lower class members, in relatively tranquil times. It accommodated new interests and classes, including underprivileged groups, by coopting their upwardly mobile leaders into the existing structure of influence and power. The limitations of the Congress system too lay in its rather narrow class and caste basis, with the system therefore being reduced to an inter-elite game of power.

The Indian parliamentry system, modelled too closely on Westminster, has become disproportionately preoccupied with the management of electoral politics, conceived to accommodate local elites in the existing framework and thus forging an electoral machine. This model keeps the poorer strata out, except as part of vote banks patterned after traditional patron-subject relations.

The Indian democracy was thus conceived and managed after independence. It need not have been conceived so. During the national movement a large number of constructive work programmes had focussed attention on not only the poor and the needy but also on those victimised and ostracised socially. They were considered as legitimate participants of the Congress movement. Indeed, the movement derived its legitimacy and broad support base from them. After independence the two parts of the movement – political and social – became divorced, and the Congress confined itself to the former. The latter was left to 'Gandhians' who were however given large grants and in some cases were incorporated and given semi-official status, for example, the promotion of khadi and village industries, and handicrafts.

The government was seen as the principal instrument of social change and this worked so long as the nationwide organisational framework of the Congress maintained a close relationship with voluntary agencies operating in rural areas and the various front organisations dealing with special segments of the population (industrial labour, dalits, tribals, women, students). When the party organisational aspect began to be assigned a secondary role, the state and district (and lower) level politics were stymied, and the various elements in the non-governmental sectors – voluntary agencies, front organisations and professional associations – became governmentalised through state patronage and political jockeying, the Congress system found itself unable to handle the overload.

The degeneration began during the Nehru period but its full consequences were felt only under Indira Gandhi. Meanwhile, completely new pressures began to surface with the advent of mass politics. Indira Gandhi was perhaps the most important catalyst of mass politics after 1969, but she was unable to fathom the institutional implications. Instead of mobilising people's aspirations and discontent through an organisational strategy that would take the Congress to the masses and make the Congress government respond to the legitimate demands and urges of the people, and contain those that were irresponsible and excessive, she chose to develop a direct, amorphous and highly personalised relationship with the masses. *Garibi hatao* and the year 1969 could have yielded a new institutional structure to the Indian state; in point of fact, it started a process of de-institutionalisation.

Another opportunity of this kind came in 1977, but again the Janata leaders were clueless and like Indira Gandhi before them, they more keen to retain their power than to build an alternative political structure. By 1980, of course, politics had lost its moral stance and all that the people were promised by the Congress when it came back to power was a 'government that worked'. But a government cannot work by itself. It needs a system, a state apparatus that is well oiled and properly orchestrated. Such an infrastructure did not exist nor was it freshly devised. Since then the situation has worsened.

Rebuilding the State

I have attempted to recapture and assess the Indian experience with democratic state and nation building in an effort to help restructure the Indian state, now in a condition of atrophy. Such an assessment, of both failures and opportunities, would provide important clues. The conception of rebuilding a viable democratic state needs to be based on such an interpretation of what has happened. Then the capacity to build on the interpretation and change the state in the light of new developments and understandings can be nurtured.

Such an interpretation would provide the criteria to restructure and innovate. The restructuring should involve the restoration of the balance between the central initiatives necessary in operating a modern state and the participatory and politicising role of the party system, local institutions and local elites. The innovation should help in the transition from the Westminster model of parliamentary democracy to new processes and structures that can channel the deep stirrings and heightened consciousness of the people.

My purpose here has been to identify alternative processes for building a viable social democratic state; provide the criteria and directions along which these processes need to be structured; and lay out a strategy for a new alignment of forces that will take these processes along new directions. Alternative model-building exercises will not lead to much unless they are seen as part of a larger political process of change and reconstruction.

The political process in India was never fully restored since its suspension in the mid 1970s. But while the mainstream political process stagnated, a new political climate was coming into existence in the wake of (a) greatly increased perception among the people of the value of politics in the struggle for social change; and (b) growing perception among grassroots activists about the need to link micro-movements of constructive work, rural conscientisation and organisation of the poor, to a macro-movement that is consciously perceived as a political process. The political process would be different from the kind in which political parties are engaged, but it would be a political process nonetheless. The task now is to make the mass stirrings and the grassroots activism the basis of an alternative political process and, as the crisis of the state deepens, make that process the catalyst of a new structure for the state.

It is absolutely necessary to link the powerful processes generated at the lower levels of the polity to a larger nationwide political process if we are to avoid the dangers of unrestrained populist politics and appropriation of its symbols and its appeal by demagogues and adventurists. We must refrain from romanticising the masses as well, least we reduce the people of India with their diverse traditions and resources to a diffuse and malleable mass that could be easily appropriated by dominant groups and vested interests.

We must not ignore the creative role of the state with its capacity to intervene in the social process and provide mechanisms for liberation from age-old inequities and exploitative strangleholds. While being critical of excessive centralisation, and stressing the value of local institutions, voluntary agencies and movements, we must also categorically reject the anti-state bias that is gaining ground. The challenge we face is of simultaneously building a viable state and a democratic social order, recognising that they have both been eroded. While the concept of democracy cannot be limited to the political arena but must extend to the socioeconomic process, it is equally true that the only manner in which democratic forces can be stabilised and strengthened is by operating through the institutional structures of a viable state.

It follows that the task before the intelligentsia, the micro-movements stirring the countryside, the middle-class conscientisers working in and through the grassroots, the mass organisations of workers, peasants and specific underprivileged strata, as well as individual political workers who find common cause with these movements, is to engage in this larger process. The need is for a *new political process* that arises from the democratic aspirations of the people, produces a *new elite* that is at once rooted and sensitive, and paves the way for *new institution building* and a *new state structure.* We need to put an end to the isolation of single constituencies – women, tribals, youth, dalits – for fear of being swamped, as well as overcome the constraints posed by individual egos and biases.

This was the strength of Gandhi's model of building from the grassroots without ever losing track of the larger national struggle. The political process that lies ahead will involve picking up the threads where Gandhi left them, which had been set aside in the almost exclusive preoccupation with operating the institutions of the state based on the Westminster model.

The tasks that await the new coalition of social forces in yoking their varied attempts towards a collective effort and providing new directions to the national polity are:

1. Replacing the present dissipated state structure and building a viable one.
2. Creating an elite that is rooted in, and is sensitive to, the aspirations underlying mass politicisation and is therefore able to relate political organisations based on class and caste lines to the institutional structures of a modern democratic state.
3. Developing new institutions that draw on the wide array of initiatives operating outside government structures in the form of voluntary agencies engaged in constructive activities, local activist groups taking up the cause of underprivileged sections and various local movements against landed and other vested interests.
4. Evolving a planning, communication and decision-making structure that operates both ways (bottom–up and top–bottom), but of which the effective catalytic levels are the various intermediate ones – between the centre and states on the one hand, and the large mass of villages on the other – through which a new multitier federal political process can be developed.

5. Moving gradually towards a new political party that is able to draw on this new coalition of forces at various levels and on that basis restructure the Indian state.

Once such an elite, committed to joining grassroots politics with national politics, emerges and makes itself felt as a political force, the call for a radical restructuring of the constitutional order can be given—a restructuring that is undertaken after careful consideration of various issues, widely discussed in the country and submitted to the people for their approval. This is the only way to fight the imposition of a plebiscitary form of democracy from above.

7

Democracy in India: Background and Emerging Challenges

As we move towards concluding the broader reflections on democracy in this monograph, let us focus on the Indian case. While I have dwelt at some length on the broad issues – both theoretical and in respect of the unfolding processes – in general terms, the background for all of it has been the Indian experience in democracy with which I have dealt over several decades. Whatever be my critique of democratic theory in general, it is to be seen against the background of the Indian experience in building a truly democratic polity. In this chapter, we will attend specifically to the Indian experience in carving out such a polity.

The Basic Challenge

Bearing in mind the diverse trends and counter-trends in India's attempt to carve out a democratic course for itself, and despite the various dilemmas it has faced, India has forged a truly democratic future for itself. This future draws upon both the traditions inherited from the past and the challenges encountered in the present—contemporary India in a state of turmoil. Two main factors are responsible for the turmoil: a broad commitment to the democratic norm on the part of large sections of society giving rise to new stirrings of consciousness and organisation; and the powerful impact of the modern theory of development on the thinking of the elite, which has produced profound dislocations in the economic, technological and resource bases of the Indian people. Every society must work towards managing the profound consequences of modern science and technology, and the doctrine of development and theory of state that have followed. It must deal with the fragmentation and centralisation inherent in modernist world view, and preserve the integrity and inner vitality of its traditions, community lifestyles and values, while fully accepting the need for change and developing the capacity to cope with change.

Contemporary India is in the throes of this challenge. Democracy provides the impulse towards change, an impulse deeply ingrained in Indian tradition and providing the leitmotif of its current awakening; an awakening that is engulfing large masses of people and informing a vast array of social movements. The political process in India is informed by the struggle between carrying through the democratic process in its fullness and the elite processes emanating from technocratic drives that militate against popular aspirations. India is still democratic; however, keeping it democratic will depend on the outcome of this struggle being waged not just at the sociopolitical but also at the intellectual and philosophical levels. The values and aspirations generated by this undertaking has run into serious obstacles arising not so much from structural or cultural impediments inherent in traditional society, but rather from the mindless pursuit of the modern development paradigm and the usurpation of community resources and lifestyles by an elite more keen on catching up with other societies than on providing an equitable and humane foundation for its own people.

The questions raised are: How has India remained democratic so far (with the exception of 1975–76)? Why, despite gigantic, socioeconomic problems and the prolonged incapacity of governments to resolve them, has democratic politics not been undermined? How has the democratic polity not buckled under the onslaught of parochial backlash, ethnic and regional separatist movements, the rise of religious fundamentalism and the persisting hold of illiteracy, poverty and backwardness? How does the Indian democracy manage to survive, despite flawed functioning and serious defects?

The questions are genuine, but they continue to be posed because of their misplaced theoretical simplicity—that there is an inherent antithesis between democracy and factors like tradition, economic backwardness, strong parochial identities and low development of indices of modernisation (literacy, urbanisation, exposure to mass media, and the spread of rationality and scientific values). If we accept such a conception of the prerequisites of democracy, India is bound to be a deviant case. Such an argument has been pursued from the right and the left of modern western thought. This argument ignores the great relevance of tradition and culture for providing depth and resilience to a democratic polity. India is a deviant case in a much more fundamental sense, in that most threats to democracy in India originate from the modern sector and its pursuit of state power. This sector steamrolls traditional pluralities in an effort to create a modern, united, prosperous and powerful polity. And yet it is only because of the great appeal of the idea of democracy for the large masses of people, steeped in tradition, that the country continues to be democratic. In the short term while India may suffer reverses, widespread civil strife and an authoritarian backlash, its future as a democracy is assured.

Rather than argue in abstract theory, I shall try to lay out the empirical basis of why I think India has remained democratic: first, by analysing elements of Indian tradition that are democratic, in the process demonstrating how the advent of modern democratic thought and the institutions of representative democracy found fertile ground in India; second, by showing how the leaders of India's anti-colonial struggle operated and institutionalised a democratic polity in the first few decades after independence; and, third, by reviewing recent strains and stresses, as well as new possibilities and prospects.

Tradition and Democracy

The most striking aspect of India's historical culture is the great variety and heterogeneity that it has encompassed and preserved. This unique nature is the result of the diversity of ethnic and religious groups that have entered the subcontinent in succession and settled down; the eclectic rather than proselytising style of spiritual integration characteristic of Indian tradition; the absence of either a unifying theology or a unifying and continuous secular tradition; and above all, a highly differentiated social system that has brought functional hierarchies, spatial distinctions and ritual distances into a manifold frame of identifications and interdependence. The consequences have been a continuous pattern of coexistence between diverse systems and lifestyles; persistence of local subcultures and primary loyalties; an intermittent, unstable and discontinuous political centre; and an essentially plural social tradition in which the government functioned as only one among many centres.

India is perhaps the only great historical civilisation that has maintained its cultural integrity without identifying itself with a particular political centre. In contrast to the great empires of history, the unity of India owed not to the authority of a given political system, but to the wide diffusion of cultural symbols, spiritual values, and structures of roles and functions characteristic of a continuous civilisation. The essential identity of India has been cultural, not political. To be sure, there always was a secular component in India's culture, and it was through the constant interplay between the secular and the spiritual that the system was able to adapt itself to changing situations. And yet, there has all along been a marked disassociation between government and society, as well as between the secular and spiritual components of civilisation. This dissociation, however, did not give rise to the ecclesiastical–temporal battles so characteristic of the west.

The interaction between the spiritual and the secular, institutionalised by alliances between the political and priestly figures, has been the chief mechanism of Indian society's absorptive capacity. It has also permitted differential and segmented change, avoiding too much aggregation, without at the same time eroding the society's faith in certain elements of its culture. In the words of J.C. Hesteerman, 'We will have to think of Indian modernity in terms of the continuity of India's ever changing tradition.' More significantly, it was because of the continuity of cultural identity that far-reaching changes in the secular sphere were easy to affect from time to time. Lack of strong identification with a given political order, the presence of a retentive base in the cultural system and the tendency to de-emphasise the importance of secular changes together led to conditions that permitted continuous adaptation to, rather than hostility towards, changes in the political sphere. The perception of a threat to the 'essence' of Indianness was very little, for the essence was not really political. In historical societies with a more continuous secular tradition and in which the dominant identification was with the political order, such changes have given rise to both prolonged resistance and a considerable sense of humiliation and defeat when they eventually did come about (as in the case of China). Viewed thus, we can see why in the most recent period, despite a strong sense of nationalism, India's political elite showed no marked hostility to the adoption of apparently alien institutions.

With reference to the functional utility of an antecedent dissociation between cultural and secular traditions, another point must be added—that both these traditions were embedded in a differentiated structure of identities, and in a world view that was not only highly permissive and accommodative but also self- consciously pluralistic. While the dissociation permitted a wide range of changes in the political sphere, the pluralistic antecedents provided hospitable ground for preservation of the Indian predilection for the autonomy of social institutions and local identities, and the tolerance of cultural and religious diversities.

Such a structuring of identities explains why the observation about new nations – that participation in national political associations and voting serves to exacerbate parochial identities – did not hold true in India for a considerable period of time. When ultimately a political system emerged at the national level, it assumed the characteristics of a new all-India cultural tradition. In time, when the new political system was dispersed and decentralised, regional and linguistic identities had emerged and these provided material for political conflict. But by then the exchange equations of the new all-India frame had been well established. A clear distinction should, therefore, be made between segmentation based on new kinds of political identity (regional or linguistic) and the antecedent segmentation provided by caste and community. The former informs the political exchanges among the higher elites while the latter provides the stuff of mass politics. Commentators who see an identity crisis in India resulting from the difficulty of transferring from parochial to national identity draw their inferences mainly from the former. They also seem to place too exclusive an emphasis on national identity, following the historical experience of the west, whereas the Indian model of identity formation is more likely to be structured through a series of intermediate identities.

The Old and the New

On the other hand, the fact that the larger identities in India were essentially cultural also meant that the new political centre had considerable freedom to maneuver; it gave rise to a new and distinctive elite, and made possible a new kind of socialisation for those who entered the political arena. The antecedent tradition of social and religious diversity contributed to the new crystallisation. But there was much that was novel in the new state, and the political and social ideologies to which it was committed. Due to the relative absence of encroachment from other centres of society, the elite in the political and intellectual centres could be socialised along new lines, made to identify with ideas and institutions that were new, even if not wholly alien, and led to undertake an ambitious design for social change. Although it sounds paradoxical, the new political order could make its inroads into society in so short a time largely because of the lack of pre-existing political identities.

There is also a deeper reason to be found in the perspective that the new elite brought to bear on its role in promoting social change. The leaders of India's independence movement and the new Indian state did not view their task as one of rejection of tradition in the name of an alien ideology. Responding to such an accommodative style the traditional elites too adapted to the new dispensation and reordered the basis of their interaction with the political sphere, while still retaining the autonomy of the social and cultural spheres. In this manner India has been able to avoid the convulsions experienced by societies with long-standing secular identities many of which started their new revolutionary careers by rejecting the legitimacy of the social and cultural spheres in a self-righteous assertion of the supremacy of the political order.

Thus, by long experience, India has learned to be tolerant of pluralism, dissent and opposition. It has displayed a high tolerance of ambiguity. Over the centuries Indians have got used to wide disparities in material comforts and in their access to positions of influence and power. Consequently they have shown a marked tolerance of deprivation and humiliation. All these characteristics of Indian tradition inform the pattern of politics in contemporary India.

The Indian Model

While economic and social changes in the Indian model of development are planned and directed from above, the changes are nonetheless carried out within the framework of an open polity. Therefore the manipulation of change, of a few dominant ideas, is conditioned by an accelerated pace of political competition, changing structures of power and influence, and widening base of political consultation and persuasion. The model is based less on coercing individuals and groups in new directions and more on permitting them to pursue their own growth, albeit within a framework enacted from above. It is based less on the transcendence of individual self-interest by reasons of state, and more on the reconciliation of such self-interest with the common good as interpreted by a legitimised elite.

Moreover, the arena of power is not limited to a ruling oligarchy or an aristocracy of birth; it is being unfurled for the society as a whole by the inclusion of new sections in its ambit. In the European case, during the phase of rapid industrialisation and social change, political participation was confined to the upper class of society. In the case of revolutionary experiments, of both communist and non-communist varieties, barring intra-party feuds and military coups, political competition is generally not allowed to interfere with the process of development. In India, by and large, politics is neither suppressed nor confined to a small elite. On the contrary, politics provides the larger setting within which decision making in regard to economic development and social change, and application of pressures for redirecting development and change take place.

For a period of time, this was not so clear. Although in theory there was adult franchise and there were a number of political parties, in practice the ruling group was small and united. With the passage of time and the activisation of the electoral process, however, diffusion and diversification in the structure of political power have assumed decisive importance for the whole process of change. More recently, with the growing failure of elected governments to deliver the goods, the political process has entered a new phase of protest movements and grassroots politics, involving the deprived masses, waged outside the regular party and electoral channels.

In short, the Indian model of development is characterised by the politicisation of a fragmented social structure, through a wide dispersal and permeation of political forms, values and ideologies. Operating against the background of an essentially apolitical society, such a process involves the building of a political centre, the diversification of this centre through a network of benefits and obligations, and the mobilisation of diverse sections of society in this network. The process culminates by closing the gap that has traditionally divided village society from the polity.

My characterisation of India as an apolitical society is based on one of its principal shortcomings throughout its long history —its inability to function politically, to construct a viable political authority. My characterisation does not just rest on some cultural predisposition. It is in this context that the enormously innovative and creative role of the modern political process becomes clear. And it is this context which shows why such an undertaking had to at once include the building of a centre and its diversification throughout the subcentres of society. Central to both, however, is the role of the political in social change. There have always been voices against assigning such a role to politics, especially against engaging in its purview the mass of the people. These voices still continue and have indeed grown stronger with the rise of a technocratic vision of managing society and the conflicts inherent in it. One major refrain has been the alleged contradiction between the need for rapid economic development and the persistence of a slow and often intransigent process of democratic politics.

One strategy of development would have been to establish and maintain over a long period of time an authoritarian structure of political leadership engaged in an undissipated administrative drive from the beginning, through a powerful bureaucracy indifferent to political pressure, and through the operation of a parallel one-party machine. Whereas modernisation of the social structure must be pursued in order to arouse and guide the party machine in new directions, political competition according to this line of thinking would have to be confined within narrow bounds. Consultation with local groups and their mobilisation in the public arena would be pursued as a matter of tactics, but there would be little reason to turn these into an ideology of political participation.

India chose not to pursue such a strategy of development. Other factors outweighed the political compulsions of centrally planned economic development. In its effort to erect a unified national political coalition and in its attempt to work out the institutional mechanics of a mass democracy the Indian leadership was forced to compromise one after another the simple-minded canons of sacrifice and austerity that it had preached during the years following independence. It chose to give precedence to the complex and difficult task of mobilising intermediate and peripheral structures through a simultaneous pursuit of integrative and participatory goals rather than simply streamlining these structures for the primary purpose of extracting a growing economic surplus for the state from the people. The latter goal was also pursued by the elite; but the strategy of achieving it was less through authoritarian manipulation and suppression than as part of a comprehensive process of social and political mobilisation.

Such an approach undoubtedly led to a great deal of groping and muddling, for there was no clear model to follow. It was, instead, an unique attempt at simultaneous achievement of political and economic development while at the same time undertaking a reconstruction of a hardened social structure. On the other hand, it is not so clear any more that the authoritarian formula necessarily works, especially in cultures where the central symbols of secular authority have not penetrated into all regions, and where sub-national identities have yet to be woven together into a viable federation. Indeed, it is more probable that the only way in which India could be ruled from New Delhi was by New Delhi establishing a coalition with the centres of sub-national identities. A preference for political participation and adult franchise, under such conditions, was not simply an act of faith; it also provided a pragmatic design for national integration and political mobilisation, and also effective economic development. At any rate, the Indian approach to nation building involved such a preference for the pursuit of simultaneous goals rather than any sequential ordering through suppression of competitive goals.

Structural Characteristics

Now we shall examine how such a cultural predisposition to democracy in India was translated into an institutional model which in turn found roots in the social structure. Again the Indian experience is in many ways unique. The key to contemporary India's institutional design is not to be found in a revolutionary overthrow of antecedent structures, or in a simple carryover of the bureaucratic apparatus built by the colonial power and inherited by the new ruling class. In India, while the 'steel framed' bureaucracy continued to be in charge of the administration after the transfer of power, the relevant power structure that prevailed for a long time after independence emanated not from the legacy of a colonial edifice but from that of the national movement. The core institutional mechanism through which the new power structure was shaped, was provided by the Indian National Congress, creating continuity from the national movement. The Congress was converted into not just a ruling party, but a dominant framework institutionalising the whole process of power. The party system that emerged from such a framework was somewhat distinctive and, as we shall see, served Indian democracy well during its period of consolidation and consensus making. We shall first go over the characteristics of the movement phase that set it apart from similar movements for independence, and then examine in some detail the principal features of the Congress-dominated system that emerged after independence. Again, as in the previous section, the emphasis will be less on the historical or institutional details of the operating structure and more on the defining features of the model that emerged. Only thus can we deal with the key question: Why has India been democratic? We shall later examine the shortcomings of the model and how, over time, it dissipated.

An essential feature of the growth and authority of the Indian National Congress, as distinct from other nationalist movements, was its consolidation over a long period of time. Established in 1885 – and even then starting on the basis of almost fifty years of renaissance and reform, and the spread of communications and education – it passed through a prolonged period of intellectual agitation when its objectives and goals were articulated and disseminated among the growing middle classes in metropolitan and urban areas. This was essentially a modernist phase, influenced greatly by British education and administrative reforms, and it took place under the framework of the British

Raj. Although it became an active organisation in the cause of national freedom, it soon led to frustration due to its narrow social base and its ultra-modern idiom of communication. It required the genius of Mahatma Gandhi to comprehend the lacunae and to try and provide a mass base to the movement. He did this by developing an elaborate network peopled by thousands of workers at various levels and a new symbolism that would bridge the great gaps that divided modern India from traditional India. This was to be undertaken without resort to any notion of pursuing a class war or even by further cultivating the high native tolerance of disparities and deprivations.

The Role of Mahatma Gandhi

Gandhi provided a concentration of charisma, resorting to traditionalist symbols of identity and cohesion that forced all the sections of the Congress rank and file to capitulate. He did this in three ways. First, he developed a model of 'exemplary' life by making his own life – including its most intimate aspects – a museum of national learning. Second, he converted large and already widely discussed dilemmas of Indian social structure into charismatic symbols: he labelled the vast masses of untouchables as *harijans* (sons of God) and launched a powerful movement to ameliorate their oppression, which became a plank for the national movement. He championed the cause of women and spoke of their liberation almost in the style of feminism. He made the symbolism of Hindu–Muslim unity a general plank of social solidarity. He made the indigenous homespun cloth (*khadi*) emblematic of all who would aspire to be nationalists, a symbolism that still continues to prevail among political cadres. He developed a comprehensive programme of constructive work in the villages, and among tribals and dalits. He rarefied traditional concepts of sacrifice and austere living into minimum qualifications for nationalist workers. He ordered the educated middle classes to go into villages and serve the people. He transformed the whole appeal and draw of individual prayer into a routine institution of the nation during which his solutions for problems of politics were highlighted and diffused.

Third, Gandhi tuned the symbolism of a pacifist, saintly India to a militant organisational style, indeed the well-knit organisational drive of the Congress, with a programme of action and a powerful identity and discipline. This enabled him to include in the Congress all streams of ideological thought and all important social interests. It gave rise to a high tolerance of ambiguity in the concerns of the national movement, allowed dissent to become part of the overall consensual style of the Congress, and imbued the Congress with great flexibility and freedom to maneuver. By providing an overriding symbolism – that had the sanction of tradition and had passed the test of functionality – he built bridges all over. Gandhi had the great gift of transforming dimensions of time (the bridging of several centuries) into concrete dimensions of space (bridging the gap between the city and the village) and penetrating both with an idiom of modernisation that had indigenous meaning, simplicity of communication and great organisational as well as personal potency. He constantly reinterpreted traditional concepts of authority, social obligation and self-realisation, and furnished them with meaning that proved functional in the development of national consensus and political identity. Above all, he wielded tremendous personal authority and created instruments for consolidating this authority – the Congress high command and the vast band of Gandhian workers – by resolving tensions and cleavages in the government through definitive solutions and formulae that could not be effectively challenged even by other popular heroes of the movement.

Fourth, Gandhi made prominent a certain consensual style in Indian tradition by grafting and reinterpreting this aspect in the context of modern politics and giving it an ideological colour by invoking labels such as 'non-violent struggle' and 'peaceful disobedience' waged by a 'servant of the people' even when he was combatting a powerful enemy. As for his own rank and file in the Congress, he emphasised the great virtue of discipline in the maintenance of political potency; he accommodated men of diverse capacities and intellectual background, and always valued the cohesion and discipline of the movement above any ideological or doctrinal considerations, or even considerations of personal pride. He even symbolised and made functional the Indian tolerance of humiliation and deprivation, and turned these into programmatic plans of 'civil disobedience' and mass imprisonment at the hands of the colonial power. All this enabled him to build a distinctive national identity and through it an authoritative structure of political organisation. It was the latter that ultimately succeeded in gaining power from the alien rulers and provided the nation with a framework of political authority.

Consensual Polity: The Congress System

When the Congress came to power after independence, it inherited a historical consensus, a considerable organisational base, and a widespread feeling of trust and confidence. It converted itself into a 'party of consensus', dominating the political landscape, enjoying legitimacy and a high sense of political efficacy. But the conditions of its future success were drastically changed. Its basis of power was no longer the authority of a few towering personalities nor the unanimous agreement to oust a common enemy. On the one hand, it had to operate through a constitutional system of government based on adult franchise and party competition; and on the other hand, it had to resolve pressing issues that could no longer be neglected. Immediate decisions were called for, and a new strategy of consensus and consolidation were necessary.

The Congress party's approach to these issues was five-fold: 1. The Congress, when it came to power, assigned positive and overwhelming roles to government and politics in the development of society. 2. The Congress made the power of the central authority the chief condition of national survival. This power was not only consolidated but also greatly augmented. 3. The Congress made legitimacy the principal issue of politics and permeated the government and the ruling party with great symbolic value. Only the Congress could be trusted. Therefore only the Congress was the party of consensus. The political system was legitimised through identification with a particular leadership, and its agents and heirs. This made the symbolism of the Congress concrete and manifest. 4. The Congress in power made for a concentration of resources, a monopoly of patronage and a control of economic power which crystallised the structure of its authority and made competing with it a difficult proposition. 5. By adopting a competitive model of development, the Congress made mobilisation and public cooperation a function of political participation rather than of bureaucratic control and police surveillance. Only the Congress, with its huge organisational legacy, its leadership and its control of institutional patronage, could provide such a framework of participation.

The Congress was able to consolidate its own power on these lines and at the same time provide the nation with a framework of authority, a diffuse ideological and programmatic consensus, a broad-based agreement on institutional and procedural forms, and a powerful symbolism of identity and affect. In this, its task was facilitated by the presence and consolidation of charismatic authority – personalised for a long time by Nehru – diffused and institutionalised through a pluralistic structure of political organisation and leadership. Although a number of political parties came to the fore after independence, the Congress was recognised as the main party, representing a historical consensus and enjoying a continuing basis of support and trust. Under the circumstances, political competition was internalised and carried out within the Congress. In the process, a system of patronage was worked out in rural India, traditional institutions of kin and caste were sought to be incorporated. Through the system a structure of pressures and compromises developed. In the course of the working of this system political competition was intensified, changes took place and new cadres of leadership drawn from a diffuse social base came to power. An intricate structure of conflict, mediation, bargaining and consensus developed within the framework of the Congress. The system got aggregated at the state level where individuals who had risen to power in the Congress organisation sometimes emerged as the chief opposition to the group in control of the government, provided an alternative leadership, exercised pressures on the ministerial group, and in many instances replaced it. Elections at various levels of the party organisation played an important role, as did the selection of party candidates for the general elections.

The role of the opposition parties in this system was to act as 'parties of pressure', operating outside the Congress but constantly criticising, pressurising, censuring and influencing opinion and interests inside the party. The Congress was itself organised into a factional continuum ranging from left to right, traditional to modern, and encompassing various regional and parochial interests, as also more secular and modern pressure groups. Furthermore, the opposition parties constantly exerted a latent threat to the Congress—that if the latter strayed too far away from the balance of effective public opinion in any region or regions, it would be displaced from power by an identifiable group or groups which already stood in a competitive relationship with the dominant party. It was an assumption of the system that the party of consensus, which was presumably the only legitimate instrument of power, was sensitive enough to public pressures and demands. But a safeguard was nonetheless provided through the operation of this latent threat so that other groups were available as an alternative to the Congress whenever the normal mechanism provided by competing elites within the party of consensus failed to respond. The system worked remarkably well and for a long period time made for considerable mobility and responsiveness both within the Congress and in terms of its competitive position vis-à-vis other parties and groups at various levels of the national polity.

The Congress succeeded in establishing its dominance and offsetting threats from other parties and groups by a progressive expansion of its social base, so that ever-new bases of recruitment and support were available to it. It could tilt a majority in its favour in most regions and continue in its position of dominance. It achieved expansion and majority using three methods, all of which were to extract their costs eventually. First, soon after independence it engaged in a process of displacement of its own elite structure. Rather than rely on its own rank and file inherited from the nationalist days and committed to its programme of reconstruction, the Congress chose the easy, and at that time efficient, course of taking the socially and economically entrenched groups into its organisation—landed gentry, businessmen, peasant proprietors, new industrialists and the rural middle class. This provided the Congress with a rough and ready structure of support, with electoral link men who controlled various vote-banks, and with a structure of consensus and authority in the constituencies. Second, the Congress initiated a process of social cooptation, supplementing the higher castes that dominated the party machine but were likely to be split into competing factions with new elite groups from middle and lower castes, thus expanding its social base and continuing its numerical ascendancy. This allowed the Congress to penetrate local regions and strongholds of traditional authority, as well as newly emergent bases for new loyalties. Third, through its extended programmes of development and planning, the Congress developed an elaborate network of patronage which enabled it to bargain political support in return for economic and social benefits for various social strata in rural and urban areas. All this enabled the Congress to be a 'catch-all' party and further consolidated its electoral organisation on the basis of the traditional social structure and the emerging structure of economic opportunities. Both the traditionally entrenched social groups and the new aspirants developed stakes in the Congress. They were inculcated the symbolism and procedures of the electoral and parliamentary systems to which the Congress had given rise, and actively involved in the overall framework of authority and decision making. The resulting distribution of consensus and affect proved highly functional to the development of democratic values and procedures among the large masses of the Indian people.

Such a process necessarily confronted the Congress with new issues and new pressures, towards which it employed approaches. On the one hand, it firmly neutralised the more glaring sources of cleavage in Indian society by timely and often anticipatory legislation—abolition of feudal and landed rights (*zamindari*), far-reaching protective labour legislation, removal of gross social inequalities by grant of special rights and privileges to depressed sections of society, linguistic reorganisation of states, and firm suppression, backed by legislation, of secessionist and violent activities in various parts of the country. Accompanying such legislation was the Congress attempt at penetration, for example, into the labour unions; and accommodation, for example, meting out special treatment to minority communities, such as reservation of Congress 'tickets' for elections. The Congress also developed an informal but elaborate system of conciliation and resolution of conflicts and factional disputes (which often reflected disputes between the Congress and the opposition parties) through the mediation of prominent individuals at various levels. Together, these steps led to a considerable strengthening of the party of consensus and a corresponding weakening of the potential sources of cleavage that could have gravely affected the framework of consensus.

However, the Congress also showed a growing tendency towards conflict avoidance, especially when the threatening issues were likely to lead to greater visibility of ideological discord, power disputes and internal disunity. It refrained from institutionalising resolution of power conflicts and preferred to keep the process informal. It shelved important issues of principle that appeared to threaten its eclectic and all-encompassing character. The Congress avoided open expression of important conflicts at public forums like the All India Congress Committee, insisted on 'unanimity' in internal elections, and often preferred short-term compromises that would help maintain the status quo than look for long-term solutions that might endanger the delicate balance on which its massive and amorphous organisation rested. It created several buffers between levels of political articulation – mediating committees for which sanction was obtained from the high command, a system of observers deputed from one level to another, and numerous informal consultative councils and inner groups in the leadership framework – that substituted for the open articulation of internal divisions and cleavages. Neutralising of potent sources of disaffection, avoidance of conflicts and consensual style of operation were instrumental in securing the national consensus represented by the Congress. At that point of time it encompassed a wide swathe of social reality which was made the basis of an eclectic and non-ideological framework and posture of political affiliation.

Supporting such a structure of consensus were two dynamic agents of transformation—charismatic power and pliable tradition. The role of Gandhi in providing personal example, moral fervour based on indigenous symbols of identity, and militant organisational style to the emerging national community have already been discussed. Gandhi was followed by Nehru who personally shaped and dominated the post-independence political system; provided it with a long period of stability and continuity; crystallised its institutional contours; imparted to it an overriding personal symbolism, pedagogy and self-confidence; and enabled the system to bear the load of an expanding framework of political participation, economic and social mobilisation, and open competition and criticism. There also emerged dozens of smaller Gandhis and Nehrus. All over the country outstanding characters came into prominence and provided a dominant style and leadership for a considerable length of time. Their word was law, they consolidated political machines encompassing large territories on the basis of their own personality and support networks, penetrated a wide array of both traditional and developmental institutions, and constantly mediated in disputes and differences. As the process especially depended on the management of conflict and distribution of patronage, it ultimately faced the strains of demands outstripping resources. At the same time it cannot be denied that during the first generation of India's politicisation as a nation these leaders provided the rallying points of political organisation and institutional consensus. They made politics the great engine of mobilisation and identity, committed wide sections of society to the new political order, widely dispersed the symbolism of parliamentary government and economic development, and socialised traditional and emerging elites into the pedagogy and the practice of a democratic polity that was also wedded to an egalitarian ideology. Their individual personalities and manipulative roles in respect of the traditional social structure laid the basis of the emerging consensus on substantive as well as procedural issues.

Such a diffusion of personal charisma and its catalytic role in social transformation were possible because of the great pliability of the structure of secular roles in Indian tradition. It became possible to utilise the symbolism of the various traditional strata of society because of the very absence of a firm and institutionalised tradition of secularism, the great ambiguity in the operative social hierarchy of caste and the tendency in Indian society to approximate social status with access to secular power. This was utilised for both providing bases for real or presumed positions in the past, for the reinterpretation of scriptural or mythical traditions in support of such claims, and for adopting new secular forms of organisation for mobilising numerical strength and providing channels for new types of identity and self-confidence. Politics authored a considerable transformation of indigenous society while at the same time acquiring internal depth and significance. Absence of a clear-cut spiritual hierarchy, a high tolerance for ambiguity and dissent, and habitual subjugation of the social structure to the demands of secular power enabled a striking reinterpretation of tradition and consequent acceptance of modern structures and styles by large sections of the people.

Modern institutions and practices were thus legitimised, and took on the characteristics of *new traditions* rather than continuing to be exotic and tension ridden for a majority of the people. As a result, the diffusion of charisma and the traditionalisation of new norms and procedures became possible. The Congress was able to do this because of its all-encompassing and de-ideologising character; its sensitivity to both the strength and maneuverability of indigenous tradition; and its accommodative and coalitional approach to individuals and social groups aspiring for power. These characteristics later turned into liabilities for the Congress, though undoubtedly its long-term contribution to national consensus is likely to survive.

The Dilemmas of Consensus

The dilemma of the Congress system of consensus was that whereas it depended on certain elements in the social environment, the processes to which it had given rise and through which the system had been consolidated, caused those elements to be undervalued. Let us examine this relationship in some detail.

Six elements the Congress system depended on may be clearly identified. First of these was the diffusion of personal charisma, relying considerably on the availability of men and women who reflected the compelling and strongly persuasive characteristics of a Gandhi or a Nehru or a Patel throughout the regions and districts of the country. With time, however, the electoral process underemphasised the role of these individuals, challenged their authority and called for a replacement of personal diffusion by institutional diffusion. The Congress system, based as it was on the informal factional network of affiliations, failed to provide this within its own framework, and forced recourse to elements outside its own margins of competence. The functioning and proliferation of the factional network also inflated the ranks of contestants far beyond available resources and raised their self-confidence in challenging the framework and discipline that the Congress had prescribed. The result was increasing incidence of internal sabotage followed by open dissidence and defections.

The second element on which the Congress relied considerably was its historical legacy, which gave it the stamp of tradition and the absorbing capacity of a powerful conservative force. A political process that emphasised the here-and-now in place of the historical and the traditional, coupled with the Congress's own growing emphasis on a futuristic ideology, diminished its historical basis of legitimacy and underscored the need for a continuous revival of legitimacy on utilitarian and performance grounds. But the inherent difficulties of a condition of scarcity and the general failure of a party of historical consensus to attend to the concrete demands of the present contributed to the negative value of the status quo ante in Indian politics.

The third element which facilitated the dominance of the Congress and its leadership was a specific consensual style that was both indigenously strong and politically functional. Once the authority of the first-generation leadership at various levels weakened, the continuance of a style that emphasised consensus and unanimity not only on the issues and values informing them, but also on procedures, exasperated the new generation of leadership. They ridiculed the glaring hypocrisy of maintaining a formal consensus in the face of constant bickering and disputes, and the need for arriving at agreements. This failure became especially costly in the key processes of power in the system of one-party dominance—the selection of Congress candidates for the general election and organisational elections within the party, as well as the composition of various committees entrusted with the task of selecting Congress candidates. The consensual style of the Congress leadership at the top led to a process of accommodation and group representation in the various committees which only resulted in deadlocks and an exasperation with the given institutional rules. The style fomented a tendency to operate outside these rules. All this led to the traumatic consequences of open sabotage, dissidence and outright defection from the parent organisation. Even while a general consensus on goals and values was widespread and indeed increasing, the failure to maintain internal cohesion through a properly organised process of competition and dispute resolution led to disaffection within the Congress, raised the confidence of dissident and oppositional groups, and threw the coalitional pattern of Indian politics out of gear.

Closely related to the consensual style was a fourth element on which the Congress relied—the accommodation of a wide variety of social groups in the traditional framework of the party.

The accomodation can be defined by two aspects we have discussed earlier: the displacement, soon after independence, of the rank and file of the nationalist movement by entrenched social and economic interests especially in the rural areas of the country; and from that as the base line, the gradual expansion of the social base of the party by cooptation of new elite groups with a view to perpetuate the party's numerical edge over other parties and groups (as well as the edge of the ruling faction above the competing factions within the party). Both these strategies paid considerable short-term benefits, but eventually backfired. The abrogation of cadres committed to the party's goals and closely identified with its institutional and programmatic characteristics in favour of individuals already well-entrenched in the social hierarchy, and commanding prestige and resources, meant that the Congress had to rely for its support on already existing lines of identity and organisation. The Congress became heavily dependent on individuals who remained within the party mainy due to the benefit they drew from its control of government and the confirmation of their traditional status derived from such an association at a time when they were otherwise threatened by the egalitarian impacts of democratic politics. Similarly, the Congress' tendency to shift its support base from one social group to another in an attempt to retain power when faced by competitive challenges, enabled politics to penetrate down the social hierarchy; but it also meant that the resources so mobilised were soon exhausted, the factional network within the party became far too involved and was constantly shifting, and the contenders for power found their chance in alternative coalitions which ultimately challenged the very system that the Congress had consolidated and dispersed. The very amorphousness and ambiguity – and lack of sharp ideological cleavages – which were the strong points of the Congress at one time proved to be liabilities; these qualities struggled for new institutional expression. The process differed from state to state and has not yet worked itself out in the more backward states, but the description here applies to all the regions of India.

The fifth element in the Congress party's approach to consensus lay in its ability to reinterpret and secularise traditional structures of hierarchical relationships and functional differentiation to serve the necessities of recruitment and political communications for building a viable support base and incorporating the fragmented structure of Indian society within the framework of a single party. This led to both a factionalisation of traditional identities and federalisation of smaller groups on the basis of a new identity and claim to recognition. Alongside and often cutting across the earlier processes of sanskritisation (emulation of brahminic practices and rituals by lower castes for recognition and mobility) and westernisation (the entry of sanskritised castes into the framework of modernity), there emerged a new and pervasive process of secularisation. Both the sanskritising and westernising groups were being secularised through their involvement in factional and electoral politics; their organisation on associational–federal grounds; and their identification with politicised symbols, and new social and economic demands. The consequences were: a) It led to the break-up of the traditional bases of cohesion and thus of composite vote-banks that could be delivered by the leaders of old. This meant a social base that would progressively become more complicated and diverse, from which support had to be mobilised. b) The disintegration of traditional loyalties and the absence of new bases of societal integration during the transition provoked new forms of parochial loyalties – regional, linguistic and based on new forms of caste organisation – that threatened the broad-based and aggregative pattern of recruitment to higher levels. The Congress grip on social reality, articulated through the authoritative link men in various regions, weakened. New forms of antagonism and new types of demands which gained potency locally together undercut the Congress hold over society. The emerging coalitional structure of the opposition parties capitalised on these local antagonisms and soon reduced the edge that the Congress had over them. Greater secularisation of politics – as a result of the competitive and demand-oriented processes that the Congress had fashioned in its drive for political modernisation and a viable support structure – ultimately confronted the Congress with a more pluralistic structure of political competition, and undermined its authoritative and consensual character.

Finally, the Congress strategy of consolidation depended more on a dispersal of power and patronage than it did on ideological appeal or organisational loyalties. The emphasis on power as the major instrument of consensus led to an intensification of factionalism in political competition, in the process splitting almost all formal organisations, political and societal, giving rise to a loose and fluid state of personal and institutional interactions, placing an exaggerated emphasis on personalities and cliques. This reinforced a communications style based on an amorphous appeal and an organisational style that relied heavily on personal influences. Political communication became general and filled with platitudes, lacking specificity of issues, inarticulate about prevailing interest cleavages, loud in rhetoric and empty in content. Similarly, the accent on patronage as a lever for maintaining political loyalties ran into negative predispositions, due to increasing demands that could not be fulfilled, and the growth of an awareness that took rewards for granted, failing to produce commensurate returns in loyalties. In fact, loyalties were determined more by positions of power and less by past obligations or any stable pattern of political identifications. Once the frame of reference shifted from competition for positions within the party to the struggle for power per se, the rules of the game lost relevance. The party system began to shed its principal character—the provision of a stable basis of political loyalties and organisation. While such a development in the nature of political organisation made for the growth of non-ideological politics and kept the temper of politics less dogmatic and more accommodative, it made political controversies sterile and retarded the growth of competition around issues and problems. When the structure of intra-party factions, so relevant to the aggregative function of politics, became enmeshed in the factionalising habit typical of a fragmented society, political affiliations lost their specificity and their role, and contributed to the disruption of social and political institutions.

Under these conditions politics becomes liable to the loss of meaning and purpose, and begins to get discredited in the eyes of the people. When this happens in a society where the political idiom has been by tradition highly moralistic the general cynicism of the public becomes sharp and bitter. The cynicism is the result of the power group failing to reflect states of opinion and interest, and giving rise to a style of politics – centralising and distant – that proves inimical to the maintenance of a stable consensus. The very instruments of political consolidation – power and patronage – begin to undermine the growth of institutional identities which alone can guarantee a deeper consolidation of national consensus.

The Crisis of Institution Building

Three conclusions follow from the preceding discussion on the weakening and fragmentation of the Congress consensus. First, the greatest failure of the Congress lay in institution building. It failed to develop a hierarchy of cadres committed to the Congress and its programme, and build autonomous organisational structures and loyalties that transcend the particularistic clusters of patronage and influence. Political and institutional consensus requires cohesion of the elite, for without such a cohesion larger identities are difficult to develop on a long-term basis. It is in this respect that the Congress party's reliance on personal charisma and an accommodative and consensual style proved to be an obstacle to the building of more viable institutional bases of authority and consensus. Its dependence on entrenched individuals and link men – in the feudal, mercantile and other socially powerful sectors – whose commitment was conditional also distracted the party from building its own autonomous institutional bases.

Second, it is clear that there is a close relationship between strength of consensus and levels of performance. Here too the Congress party's failures after the first few years are glaring. So long as there was some approximation between the distribution of perceptions in regard to the system's efficacy and the distribution of expectations from the system, there was hope among the various sections of society which had cemented their loyalties to the Congress. Once, however, the Congress' preoccupation with holding power and holding together its own constituents began to overwhelm its concern with public problems and their amelioration, it ceased to be the party of hope, partly from the viewpoint of the people, but mainly from the viewpoint of the political elite which had to perform crucial representative functions and answer a growing tide of criticism and disaffection.

Third, the Congress through its sheer power and authority for nearly a generation had undoubtedly created a widespread base of support for democratic institutions. What has been challenged since is the utility of the peculiar party system that was dominated by the Congress, not the values and procedures, and not even the programmes and policies initiated by the Congress. Indeed what is striking is that in about all the states where the Congress was replaced from power – including states where the communists assumed power – the broad policies and programmes pursued are very much the same as those initiated by the Congress; even the style of pursuing them has not changed significantly.

It is the structural basis of authority through which the consensus articulated by the Congress has to be promulgated that has changed. This is not a slight change. Authority, its stable ordering, and respect for it are essential ingredients of any system of consensus. Failure to provide stable governments, to attend to the urgent tasks of performance, to maintain respect for authority and to demonstrate the value of politics in managing the affairs of society can lead to severe disenchantment and the search for an alternative. The dilemma of the decline of the Congress system of authority lies in the fact that the change to a new system is more symbolic than real, as all the disadvantages of the Congress from the point of view of nation building – factionalism, reliance on personalised support, pluralistic and parochial basis of organisation, and loose coalitional networks of power – are likely to continue, perhaps get magnified. The authority and discipline that the Congress framework had provided, in however attenuated a form, will be lacking. The great issue of India's transition to another party system is to produce in some measure a dominant elite that will set the tone of the national consensus; provide the organisational skills and authoritative sanctions for its institutionalisation; provide a structure in spite of the ambivalence; and contain the sources of tensions and anomie that are bound to emerge from the articulation of an even more pluralistic polity. The issue is underlined further because of the absence of alternative authoritative systems and traditions of respect and reverence for them; such as the bureaucracy, the economic technocracy, or indeed even the military. The dimension that threatens India's consolidation as a nation the most is that of time; this is likely to be even more difficult to preserve in the transition after the Congress period of dominance than was the case under the

Congress. Seen in this light the problem takes on the character of a tragic dilemma: just at a point when the system had reached the brink of success, a major upheaval in institutional and authoritative arrangements has started, and it is likely to take some more time before a new basis of stability and a new respect for authority emerge. Much would depend on the ability of the central authority to evolve a framework of sharing power and on that basis run its writ in the various regions.

The Indian National Congress represents a case study in transitional or *interim* consensus. It lacked the comprehensiveness of a more plural order but nonetheless provided a firm base in terms of legitimacy and authority of the regime; it also proved highly effective in propagating the norms and procedures of a democratic political system. On the other hand, a dynamic dissenting element was a distinct possibility in such a consensus —an element more pervasive than the usual differences and disagreements involved in a functioning consensus. It is the capacity to creatively respond to this process of rising dissent and protest movements, while stemming the decline in respect for authority, that now poses the great challenge to India's emerging polity.

Political consensus is an ongoing process, it has to be revived constantly and provided new depths. It depends considerably on the organisational skills of elites and a widespread respect for their authority. Democracy in new nation states poses both an opportunity and a threat to the process of consensus. The dilemma is nowhere so manifest and vivid as in the case of India.

The Movement for Redemocratisation

I consider the new turmoil among the Indian masses and the new forms of protest and struggle waged by a new set of actors as part of the continuing commitment to democracy, indeed to its deepening and broadening. They need to be located in the larger context of a world in transformation. They need to be understood as part of a whole range of attempts at redefining the content of politics by the hitherto peripheral and marginalised strata of a large number of societies. They need to be seen as expressions of new stirrings and responsibilities, an urge to find new creative spaces in a fundamentally conflict-ridden social situation in which avenues of participation have been cornered by a few.

Above all, these movements need to be related to the startling incapacity of regimes and power structures (parties, unions, development agencies) in coping with the new agenda of aspirations and aggrandisements. They need to be seen as a response to a growing hiatus and vacuum in existing institutional frameworks, to a felt crisis in human arrangements in the wake of new stirrings and sufferings, to a situation of growing conflict between pressures for widening the range of politics and equally powerful pressures for its contraction. They have emerged at the start of a new and different phase in the structure of world dominance, a changed situation in the nature and role of the state in national and subnational settings, and a drastically altered situation in the relationship between the people and what we term 'development'.

These movements also signify a new understanding of the democratic process which has moved from an almost exclusive preoccupation with parties and elections to deeper currents the prevailing political system has been unable to grapple with. The period of erosion of parliamentary party and federal institutions, and decline of authority of the state and national political leadership, has also been a period of the rise of new actors, new forms of political expression and new definitions of the content of politics.

Who and what are these new actors, forms and definitions? There is, first, the resurgence of the people themselves, both in consciousness and in behaviour. They are asserting their democratic rights and challenging the established order, at local levels to begin with, but affecting the entire social and political order. Though they are by no means close to transforming it. There is, second, the emergence of a new social class of mediators in the political process—the activists. They are upper and middle class in their social origin, but identify themselves with the lower orders of society—the poor, the oppressed and the segregated; social strata ranging from the untouchable castes and the destitute among the tribes and ethnic minorities, to the victims of sexual, ecological and generational discriminations, atrocities and violence.

With regard to new political expressions, there is, first, a new form of voluntarism that is not non-political. It is political in a manner different from those of parties. It aims not for the mere seizure of state power, but the redefinition of the meaning of politics, and concepts like revolution and transformation. And there is, second, a new genre of 'movements' that, while having an economic content, are in practice multidimensional. They cover a large terrain—the environmental movement, the women's movement, the civil liberties movements, movements for regional self-determination and autonomy, and the peasants' movement; and the growing movements for peace, low military budgets and an anti-hegemonical stand vis-à-vis India's neighbours.

The redefinition of politics thus, again, has many aspects. First, it is an attempt to counter the strong tendency towards depoliticisation spurred by a populist leadership under which growing numbers of people are being marginalised both from organised politics and from the organised economy. Second, it is an attempt to widen the range and arenas of politics, taking it beyond electoral and legislative politics which have led to a virtual exclusion of the mass of the people from the processes of power. Third, it is a redefinition of the content of politics so that fields of human activity that were considered outside its scope are being recognised as political. These fields provide new arenas of controversy and struggle.

The most outstanding instance is, of course, the women's movement which has brought forth deeply personal and hitherto socially tabooed relationships into the political arena. But there are many other instances, for example, the issue of public health hitherto confined to experts, the issue of rights over forests and community resources so far kept out of the public realm by their exclusion from the more 'scientific' conceptions of ecology and technology. Today the state of health and nutrition of millions of people and the disastrous ecological consequences of imported models of development for the very survival of peoples and cultures have come to occupy the attention of the new activists and movements.

Implicit in these new movements is a conception of politics and the public arena that – like the new radicalised conceptions of science and arts, and similar to the older conception of life in its great diversity – is multidimensional. These struggles are no longer limited to economic or even political demands, but seek to cover ecological and cultural issues as well. They include a sustained attack on sources of internal decay and degeneration. All of which is reminiscent of the freedom struggle in which liberation and *swaraj* were sought not just from an external power but also from the enemy within. A distinctive conception of democracy will have to encompasses the many facets and diversities of a complex social reality, without falling prey to the homogenising and oppressive thrust of the modern state, economy and technology.

8

Democracy, Participation Theory and Growth of the Non-party Political Process

Following the broader critique of democratic theory and the institutions of parliamentary and party politics, in recent decades there has emerged an alternative perspective on the basic theoretical postulates of democracy and the institutional embodiment thereof. In my own work this has been expressed in terms of the growth of non-party political process. During the same period, the concept of political society has been put forward by Partha Chatterjee, dealing with a series of social interactions and political engagements which take place outside the framework of formal institutions of the state, which are not accomodated adequately by the notion of civil society. The formulation on grassroots initiatives that emerged in the writings of D.L. Sheth deal with broader dimensions of the organisation of political power from the perspective of democratic resurgence among the people.

I. Overview: Crisis in the Theory of Participation

When I first wrote on the theme of participation in 1984, I had in mind a set of issues different from the questions raised as part of the growing interest in the conception of civil society. I had in mind the crisis that has overtaken the concept of participation in liberal theory following the rise of populist politics. Politics of this kind have been conducted in the name of people's participation, especially the poor and deprived sections of society, but in effect they have led to a process of depoliticisation, seriously affecting the participation of those very sections which were demanding a share in power and resources. Around the same time, in the 1980s, a certain importance came to be given to the model of development as conceived in the western academia. Known then as the Truman Doctrine, it gave rise to a major paradox of the age of participation. While it argued for an increase in the availability of resources for the populations of developing countries, it further strengthened the populist rhetoric – this time internationally ordained through 'foreign aid' and 'technical assistance' provided by the richer countries – fashioned to further depoliticise people in both the North and the South. The doctrine distanced people from both the organised economy and organised politics while increasing bureaucratic intervention, national and international, by communication and mass media experts and the technocratic elite. Despite these factors faith in participation remained quite large and percolated down to the mass of the people.

Contrary to the general impression that the non-party political process is a theoretical construct tangential to the mainstream development of party politics, it needs to be seen as integral to the emerging political process, in India as well as other countries. The crisis of participation has deepened since the decline of the pluralistic model of the Congress system that had provided a broadly democratic framework of governance – at the centre, in the states and also in diverse local units through coalitions of various factions – and the continuing lack of a viable democratic alternative to the Congress. In the vacuum created by the erosion of the broad social coalition provided by the contest between the Congress and its socialist, communist and decentralist oppositions, a highly fragmented and often divisive system of wielding power emerged, without providing for an all-India, macro-framework of power and institutions.

The Agenda-for-India Initiative

Several experiments were undertaken to answer the need for a real alternative to not just the Congress but to the very system based on political parties. One such experiment was the 'Agenda for India' produced by a number of intellectuals, journalists and other leading individuals some of whom had at one time played a role in the party and parliamentary systems. The broad results of the discussions and debates generated by these groups were published in the journal *Seminar*. Although this effort generated a good deal of interest while the issue was being put together during the period of the Janata government, by the time it was published Indira Gandhi had returned to power (1980). She was unwilling to listen to a group of academics and journalists who were known to have opposed the Emergency. The effort got lost in the quicksand of party politics. The other shortcoming of this effort was that it was conceived to help produce correctives to the prevailing system rather than to fashion a wholly new alternative. This made the effort appear to be a set of proposals for the ruling party, or for the opposition. It did not attempt to think afresh on the situation facing the country in terms of fresh ideas and a new set of institutions. This proved to be a disadvantage, and led to declining interest even among the intelligentsia.

The Lokayan Idea

Soon thereafter some of us organised a set of consultations at the Centre for Study of Developing Societies (CSDS) and at Lokayan. These institutes had in fact been formed in order to provide occasions where academics, activists involved in diverse struggles and policy-makers could engage in 'dialogues' that dealt with the erosion of the democratic process that began with the Emergency. This in course of time led to the conception of the broad idea of the non-party political process. There was a shift from the Agenda-for-India initiative to the formulation of the non-party political process. Whereas the former was a sociopolitical alternative to the governing structure, within the broad canvas of party politics, the latter represented an independent *societal* initiative undertaken by a set of intellectuals and activists, and laid out in leading journals, a few organs of the mass media, in academic forums, as well as through the influential writings of some intellectuals. The process took place within political parties and through existing organs of public opinion, in and beyond the mass media, in English and various other languages. It is noteworthy that even the All India Radio (presumably controlled by the government of the day) reported on both the Agenda-for-India initiative and the discussions that led to the idea of the non-party political process.

Participation in Liberal Theory

Basic to the liberal perspective has been the growth of the concept of participation. But with the advent of the concept of development liberal theory has over time moved from the pursuit of a liberal polity to the almost wholesale acceptance of the model of development. Soon thereafter took place the rise of populist politics and populist economics. Despite their impact faith in participation continued and percolated down to the people. This gave rise to a basic contradiction—the appeal for this faith among the people grew while at the same time there was a growth in popular misery and degradation. The real paradox from this contradiction is that the more the misery of the masses, the more the faith in this model of participation. In spite of the erosions in the sociopolitical framework of participation, the symbols of people's participation continue to be retained; they have become the rituals of a plebiscitary democracy. In effect, like development, participation also legitimises centralised governance and leads to dismantling of intermediate structures. It leads to a model of centralisation that increases the coercive use of the institutions of the state, effectively establishing a regime of law and order.

II. The Role of the State

In 1984, while writing about the nature and role of the state, the most critical dimension I dealt with was the gradual withdrawal of the dominant elite from the institutions of the state at a time when an extension in the role of the state would have led to its opening out to the people and their demands for a wider distribution of power and resources. Instead the state began to be perceived as an agent of technological growth with a view to catch up with the developed world, with little regard paid to the pressing needs and demands of the people at large. As regards the relationship between the state and civil society, far from being useful to the masses it has led to further exclusion in a period of economic stagnation and political instability. With this erosion in the role of the state not only the poor but even middle class professional, economic and political strata seem unable to wield authority in a meaningful way. At best they are pawns in the hands of forces beyond their control. The state itself is on the decline, its mediating role replaced by the direct rule of local landlords and dominant castes. The power of moneyed interests is on the increase, protected and enhanced by a new breed of corrupt politicians, bureaucrats and police officers. This has led to a sharp decline in the rule of law, a parallel decline in the authority of the elected governing elite, and a gradual erosion even in the power of hitherto dominant individuals and social groups such as the upper castes. Alongside, we are witnessing the rise of new fundamentalisms of religious sects, and with that the growth in power of organisations like the Rashtriya Swayamsevak Sangh, the Vishva Hindu Parishad and the Jamaat-e-Islami. The basic result has been growing communalism *within* secular politics and, as a direct consequence of that, a decline in the politics of socioeconomic transformation.

These factors have caused changes in the character of the state, making it less democratic, less secular, less institutionalised, and based less on concern for the people. Paradoxically even the concept of the grassroots has been transformed—a term that was used for socially empowering the people in a left-of-centre framework was hijacked to serve the agents of religious fundamentalism. Inevitably, the model of planned economic development was thrown overboard. Instead, a new structure emerged, constituting middlemen and lumpen professionals. And with it also grew the lumpenisation of the production process itself, leading to the growth of the unorganised sector of the economy, consisting mainly of migrants, women and children. The process of withdrawal by the people and even political agents – a withdrawal not only from organised politics but also from the organised economy – has contributed to the growth of the unorganised sector. Such a reversal of so-called participation leads to growing vacuums in the organisational structure of the state. It also leads to the depoliticisation of the people, increasing their sense of insecurity and isolation.

Inevitably all this has resulted in the decline of the role of the state, and with it of democracy and development. In place of the state new actors have emerged engaging in corruption and criminalisation, repression and intimidation. For the people, their very survival depends on their staying out of the political process, at a time when their desperate economic state makes them incapable of entering the ongoing economic process. And yet, while they are kept out of both political and economic processes, they are told that it is for them that development is taking place. If poverty persists or worsens despite development it is because of extraneous factors such as corruption or lack of adequate capital, or problems like oil price and the arms race caused by outsiders. The reality is quite contrary to what such arguments propose. It is based on growing depoliticisation on the one hand and the growth of populism on the other. The populism is fashioned in a such manner that it reinforces the emerging thrust towards depoliticisation, resulting in the growing exclusion of large masses of the people and the dispensability of the people vis-à-vis the power play of party politics.

The curious combination of the continuing exclusion of the people from the mainstream and the insistence on their participation has created a situation in which people's rights are reduced to rituals of democracy. It is a democracy that has become an instrument of populism and has assumed a plebiscitary form. Such an approach emphasises the role of the leader who is supposed to closely identify with the people and, at certain times at least, succeed in swaying their minds. One such occurrence was Indira Gandhi's call of *garibi hatao.* This leads to yet another paradox of participation: the greater the withdrawal of power from the people, the more direct becomes the relationship between the leader and the masses. The net result is that participation too legitimises centralised governance and downgrades local and intermediate structures.

With the decline in the role of the state, the role of civil society also dissipates, following the growth of economic stagnation and political instability. Paradoxically, even the bearers of state power, those who were in charge of governments, begin to lose their authority before the onward march of technology and hegemonical forces like globalisation. The concept of grassroots activism is not any longer confined to campaigns and movements for empowering the people, it is increasingly utilised by forces that undermine the political role of the state. This is perhaps the greatest paradox responsible for the growth of religious and communal outlooks. In sum, (a) the role of the state is in decline, (b) development has led to a striking dualism of the social order, (c) democracy is becoming the playground for corruption, criminalisation and repression of large masses of the people, and (d) all of the above listed factors play into the hands of outside hegemonical forces.

III. International Context

Let us look at the evolving role of the international order in undermining the nation state and the politically active elements in it—ranging from those in charge of governments and parties, to the intermediate and local bodies of both territorial and functional layouts, and to the mass of the people. Much of this has to do with the nature of the capitalist system, particularly in the changed context of corporate capitalism. Under this new version of capitalism, the resources of the third world are manipulated as part of that very effort to regulate the flow of capital to the developing economies, while in fact undermining real self-reliance and delinking the production process in these countries from the dominant countries of the North. Ideologically too, such an impact from the North is undermining the alternative strategies pursued in the South for fulfilling basic needs, ensuring national self-reliance, and raising employment opportunities and standards of health and nutrition. Such a model of participation, now cast on a global scale, only serves to undermine the stability and integrity of the production process in the third world. The growth of international pressures on the third world has led to a world scenario that is beset by an ever-growing battle for survival—of achieved lifestyles versus sheer physical survival; of corporate power structures versus the survival of states and cultures; of peace and dignity for millions of people versus persistence of structures of dominance and monopoly for ruling elites. Such a world scenario leads to a sense of desperation at both ends of the power structure, global and national, in turn leading to an erosion of the democratic polity. It gives rise to a political culture in which politicians and the bulk of the people are asked to stay away from politics.

The question is: Are the people, especially in the third world, accepting such a withdrawal from the political process? The answer is: Fortunately not. All over the world there is evidence of turbulent consciousness among large sections of the deprived. They had for long believed in the declared promise of the elites that they would in the end benefit from the system. It is only when they found the promise to be an illusion that they began to wage a struggle against those who hold the power in the system. This is particularly evident in India. The struggle arises partly out of the decades-long normative revolution generated by the adoption of democracy in a society based for centuries on the principle of inequality. And partly due to the erosion of faith in the idea of development that was supposed to make opportunities available to the mass of the people. It is generated above all by the crushing weight of the indignities, violence and deceit experienced by the poor and the dispossessed. Successive governments and different political parties have greatly reinforced the disillusionment. It has led to widespread discontent and despair which may still be highly diffused and unorganised. But the discontent is without doubt producing a growing awareness of rights; an awareness which is being felt politically and expressed politically. Whenever there is a glimpse of a prospect of mobilisation – political as well as economic – of the people, this consciousness finds an expression. It does meet resistance from powerful vested interests that refuse to shed or even share the privileges they enjoy. And yet the assertion of rights by the people continues. The result is a growing contest at the level of consciousness and political action. The consciousness is fundamentally against the paradigm of a society that is deliberately indifferent to the plight of the poor and the destitute often driven to thresholds of hunger and starvation, betrayal and humiliation.

The real failure is not just of the government in power. It is more a failure arising out of the default of the very system we have, including (a) the operation of parliamentary democracy through party competition; (b) the mixed economy composed of both the large state-owned sector and the growing corporate sector, both of which have failed to generate opportunities for the people; (c) the agrarian and forest economy that has ceased to produce food for the people and is dominated by commercial interests and corrupt politics; (d) the science and technology establishment lacking in internal dynamism and increasingly dependent on imported ideas and technology; (e) the military establishment that apart from making more and more demands on the country's resources is also called upon to perform police functions, often spreading terror in some parts of the country; and (f) the judiciary and press that may be trying their best to intervene against the growing repression of the poor, the minorities and women but are unfortunately transforming into mechanisms diffusing discontent and preventing confrontation on behalf of the establishment.

The failure of the system runs much deeper. First, the various instruments of the system – parliament, the planning commission, the executive arm – are simply unable to handle a considerably changed agenda of tasks and expectations. Second, it is a failure of the system in the sense that established opponents of the ruling elites – opposition parties, leftwing intellectuals, trade unions, cooperatives of the landless – cannot cope with such an agenda. At the same time, large numbers of people stand to benefit from this failure of the system. For example, the middle class whose parasitic lifestyles are sustained under such a system; and the numerous lumpen elements employed at the lower rungs of an ever-growing bureaucracy and a political system that relies on mercenaries.

Crisis of Theory

Above all, such a failure of the system is embedded in a crisis of theory. Both the liberal conception of the market being the arbitrator of interests and the later social democratic theory based on the positive role of a welfare state committed to equity are of little value today. Nor does the more radical socialist stream of thought of marxism provide a clear guide to action, particularly in a society in which the working class should have exercised a major role. Instead, a combination of stagnation in the rural economy and a technology that inhibits employment in the urban areas, have together lead to a situation where large segments of the population live on the margins. This in turn has produced strife and conflict *among* the lower classes.

Theoretical models that may have been of use in other cultures and societies are of little use in a sociopolitical context where poverty is taking totally new forms, where the linkage between progress and poverty has become organic and almost irreversible. Hence also the growing irrelevance of all theories of participation. What we have is a steep decline in leadership and moral values, on the one hand; and the poverty of theory as a guide to action, on the other. The result is an intellectual and moral vacuum which is then filled up by (a) populist rhetoric (taking the place of theory), (b) corruption and repression (taking the place of politics), and (c) growth of charisma which camouflages factors (a) and (b) so that there is hardly any sense of failure or crisis, especially among the ruling class.

IV. The Political and Ideological Contexts

The broad theme of people's movement and grassroots politics can be discussed against the larger political and ideological context. It is a context in which an increasing number of people are being marginalised, science and technology are turning anti-people and development has become an instrument of the privileged class.

The state, meanwhile, has already surrendered its role as an agent of transformation, or even mediator, vis-à-vis civil society. It is also a context of massive centralisation of power and resources; the centralisation is not limited the the level of the nation, in fact the nation state is itself an abject onlooker of a global order. It is also a context in which the party system, the democratic process and even the regular functioning of bureaucracy are declining and are being replaced by a new set of actors.

The revolutionary parties on the left have been contained in this political and ideological context, and where the traditional front organisations for radical action – the working class movement and the movement of a militant peasantry led by left parties – are in deep crisis. The crisis is to the growing hiatus between even these parties and their front organisations and the lower classes. The very poor are no longer attracted by the received wisdom of the left parties, but they are facing a massive backlash from established interests through measures (legislative and otherwise) aimed against them. They are also experiencing a steep rise in the repression and terror practised on them.

Growing international pressures and conditionalities to integrate the organised economy into the world economy have ended self-reliance. Millions of people have been removed from the organised economy. They have been left impoverished, destitute, drained of their own resources and deprived of minimum requirements of health and nutrition. They have been denied entitlement even to critical variables like water and shelter.

It is in response to this overarching crisis in the human arena – a crisis as much in theory as in the arenas of political action and the institutional arena based on the spaces provided by the state – that there have emerged new types of movements at various levels, demanding new instruments of political action. These movements are being spelt out in terms of grassroots politics and the opening up of alternative spaces outside of the party and the government. They involve new forms of organisation and struggle meant to transform the nature of the state and make it once again an instrument of liberation from the exploitative structures that trap the people. These movements are redefining politics at a time when several attempts are being made to narrow its range. They are redefining the basic conception of political activity—it is no longer confined to the capture of state power, it is now seen as an alternative means to intervene in the processes of history.

The emerging scenario of both decline and cooptation of what was once considered progressive and revolutionary politics provides the most relevant reasons for the rise of the non-party political process. Moreover, there are also signs of many entities which used to play a well-defined role relenting—states, parties, party-like organisations, voluntary agencies, NGOs, the organised economy and the leadership. They are relenting at a time when global, national, regional and local status quos are on an offensive; when new waves of fanaticisms are on the upswing; when governance is being destabilised and politics being depoliticised; when there is a basic crisis in the very enterprise of knowledge and in the social sciences which are gradually reaching a point of irrelevance; and when there may not yet be an end of ideology though there is a major vacuum in the realm of ideas in the traditional forums of intellectual activity.

Interestingly the growing diffusion and fragmentation of the democratic process are not all a result of conflict of ideas and personalities; they seem to be built into the very process of transformation. Part of the problem lies in the multiple arenas of problems and oppressive structures. The traditional institutions of the state, political parties and voluntary agencies are unable to respond. Nor is there *as yet* much confidence that non-party formations will succeed where others have failed. The questions that need to addressed are: How do we inject new energy and confidence into the very large mass of young and concerned citizens on whose shoulders the new challenges are likely to fall? How do we *rekindle* the creative impulse which is bound to be there in an age of turmoil? What should be the agenda of action for these new bearers of the human enterprise? How is a new strategy of transformation to be evolved through them, particularly when it is the world middle classes that are becoming conscious of their power, and are impinging on the struggling masses which are disorganised and possibly form a doomed non-class?

We need a strategy and an agenda that emerges from the here and now, empowers the people and inspires confidence among those involved in new forms of action relevant in an era of the growing disorganisation of the mass base. Mere survival calls for struggle. And, on the other hand, any long-drawn-out struggle for a better future entails the survival—of the people at large, of activists, of intellectuals, of the bearers of new democratic institutions. They would work towards sustaining and strengthening the democratic process in a way that make it an instrument of the poor.

There is no ground for romanticism or even of unguarded optimism. We cannot afford to be mere optimists, though we need to recognise that a consciousness is emerging that is serious and genuine, at various locations at many levels. It may still be weak, fragmented, lacking in resources and infected by all kinds of organisational and theoretical crises. What we need, that perhaps is already under way is a new genre of political activity, carried out in different and settings and firmly rooted in the scenes of action.

Symbiosis

Perhaps a combination of non-party and party-like organisations would help in dealing with a situation of growing despair and disenchantment among the mass of the people. Such a combination should involve movements for regional autonomy and decentralisation, including in it the involvement of regional parties that have dramatically materialised on the Indian scene. While it may be too early to assess the significance of these regional parties, there is no doubt that they represent strong expressions of the will of the people and their rejection of the ruling establishments at both the level of the region and the nation. The regional phenomenon in India may well be a composite of the rejection of the authoritarianism of the centre, the dominance of the metropolitan regions, the cultural hegemony of bourgeois cosmopolitanism, the political economy of corruption and the chauvinistic drive of the dominant elite. The multiple rejections need to be understood and dealt with as a necessary part of engaging in a larger democratic process. For in reality they too will be taking the political fulcrum close to the grassroots, providing local responses to national crises. To that extent, they become available for use in a variety of micro-movements and in the macro-politics of the non-party process.

Along with these various upsurges – the non-party political process, the regional manifestations, the search for alternatives to the prevailing system – is the crying need for reordering the distribution of power to favour the lower reaches of society and to encourage growth in the peripheries of new party forms. Whether these be upsurges in Assam, Jharkhand and the Northeast as a whole, or of left politics in Andhra Pradesh, or of a neo-nationalist upsurge in Kashmir, the fact is that the political parties involved, national or regional, are found to be engaged in carrying politics to the lower levels of the polity. They are raising completely new issues of language and culture, dignity and self-esteem, simultaneously placing emphases on mass education, employment and ecology. They are also engaging in battles against the drainage of power and resources from the local to the national. All these represent important happenings in an otherwise highly centralised state and must be taken note of by grassroots activists and movements. Contrary to party forums coopting non-party formations, as was the case earlier, it is now the turn of the latter to find common grounds with new types of party formations. There is a common need for fresh thinking on a series of issues and policies affecting the mass of the people.

V. The Micro and the Macro

The grassroots phenomena has to address the dynamics of the micro and the macro. There are two criticisms levelled against the non-party action groups and movements. First, they do not represent any basic change in the political process and are to be looked upon as at best a transition to a period when left parties will once again resume their revolutionary role and capture state power. Second, to the extent they succeed, their success is limited to local situations so that the transformations they provide for fall short of being macro—either at the national or international levels. Both these arguments appear closely related and, in a period of growing self-doubt, may find conviction even among the activists.

The need for new forms of organisation and political expression in the larger context of a world in transformation should to be understood as part of a wide range of attempts at redefining the content of politics by the marginalised and oppressed sections of society. They need to be seen as new stirrings of consciousness engulfing large masses of the people. They represent a new conception of rights and responsibilities that urge us to find creative spaces in a conflict-ridden social situation. Above all, they need to be recognised as constituting a response to the striking incapacity of regimes and power structures in coping with people's aspirations.

The non-party organisations and movements also need to be seen as comprising a response to growing polarisations and emerging vacuums in the existing framework of institutions, to a felt crisis in human arrangements. For they have emerged at a time of shifting foci in the structure of world dominance, substantial alterations in the nature and role of the state in national and regional settings, and a drastic change in the relationship between the people and what has been called development.

Therefore the rise of non-party politics has to be seen not as a transient answer to contingent situations but rather as a new historical phenomenon, playing a completely new social role and occupying a specific political space. If we are unable to explain the phenomenon in terms of existing political theory or ideological concepts, the need is to recognise the theoretical lag instead of trying to explain away the phenomenon because it does not fit received theory. Today's oppressed classes need to wage their struggles from outside the existing structures, not just by dethroning the ruling class and smashing the state, but by redefining the very concept and structure of politics with a view to empower people and transform society.

Our analysis so far, drawn mainly from the Indian experience and its global context, suggests that the phenomenon of the non-party political process has a more general relevance in the form of a response to a historical situation, though there are variations in local contexts and parameters. In fact, in my view these variations are significant in shaping the world we live in. Our empirical as well as theoretical understanding requires that the formulation 'global problems, local solutions' is not a mere cliché. We ought to know enough about the micro–macro dualism we live in to be able to say that there are no global solutions to global problems. Indeed, enough has been said in this chapter to suggest that those who work for local solutions are not bereft of a macro-perspective. A global vision is not the monopoly of the global intellectuals or the global managers of power. In fact there is reason to think that it is the global managers who are bereft of perspective or vision.

Understood in the specific sense of the politics of transformation, the macro and the micro are only differential expressions of the same process. They are not polar opposites in a pyramidal structure; rather they are coexisting contexts for variations and diversity, each autonomous and all interrelated. It is difficult to predict at what point the macro-permutations take off. It could well be a mere capture of state power. But we have argued that even the issue of state power needs to be viewed against the redefinitions of the politics of institution building, and of the role of diverse classes in the process, together contributing to the emerging politics of transformation.

A dogged confrontation is taking place between transformation and backlash; between the scenario of destitution and brutalisation and the rise of new experiments; and between a sustained struggle for a better world and the gaining of critical spaces in the expansion of the role of politics. In all this, there are grounds for creating a new society and polity out of the ruins of the old, for releasing creative spaces and for people to take charge of their lives. In the words of the French social critic Jacques Ellul, it is in times of abandonment that the need for hope finds expression.

New Impulses

The challenge now is to sustain new creative impulses and make *them* the harbingers of revolutionary change. History suggests that it is precisely in times when forces struggling for change are strongly oppressed by the established order that the will and the desire for change become heightened and the upsurge of consciousness seeks new forms of expression. As existing organisations disintegrate or lose relevance, people's activity finds fresh expression, spurred by new understandings of the historical process, and invigorated by new visions provided by individuals critically intervening in that process. These individuals may be intellectuals, or young activists, or even an alternate breed of politicians. The motivation will occur essentially at local and regional sites, and from there, given will and effort, be disseminated throughout the wider political space.

We need a review of ideological positions on a variety of themes—state, technology, revolutionary vanguards, etc. The relevant macro-positions then would inhere in political entities that transcend both the very local and the very global. We do not yet know what these entities will be; how they will cohere; how far they will take on state-like features; and the extent of their new formations, in content and style, at various levels of political expression. These are questions pertinent to the discussion of both the non-party political formations and other likely emergent forums. They are equally pertinent to the discussion on alternative approaches to the human condition, and to a consideration of the relationship between organisational forms and ideological content. These together will lead to a new agenda of both theory and action.

9

On Democracy: A Critique

Basic Critique

While examining the promises and pitfalls of democracy we have raised some pertinent questions about its capacity to satisfy people's expectations. We appear to be up against a dialectic situated in a period of rapid social change whose basic characteristics are not clear. The consequence is that democracy remains no more than an aspiration—a hope to be realised than a concretely achieved condition. Democracy is more a dream residing in the minds of philosophers and visionaries, not so much practised by those in charge of the affairs of society. It is at best pursued by theoreticians seeking the deeper stirrings of nations and states.

Our expectations from democracy far exceed what it is in practice able to deliver. These expectations are beyond the strict confines of the formal apparatus of governance called democracy. We expect to realise other goals and values—equality, freedom, peace, and minimisation of strife and violence. So much is expected from democracy even though the prevailing reality is full of ironies. Democracy is unable to deliver even within its immediate realm of being accountable to parliament and the people. It is far less able to become a catalyst of realising other values. Democracy is also expected to deliver social justice, in its full ramifications, by opening out towards new potentialities of creative intervention in the social process and the psycho-cultural domain. And yet, it is also true that without simultaneously realising these values and new potentialities, there is no point discussing democracy—what it represents, and what is inherent in it. It is a paradox that democracy has become important in providing legitimacy to regimes (even dictators commit themselves to restoring the prerequisites of democracy in seeking legitimacy) and yet, democracies are observed to be continuous arenas of strife exhibiting erosion of basic values with respect to satisfying people's aspirations and promoting goals like peace and justice.

The arenas of strife that seem to overpower the basic values are found especially in the economic sphere, following the rise of capitalism over the last century and a half. There has existed an element of mutual antipathy between democracy and capitalism ever since human consciousness in general and people's struggles in particular began challenging the capitalist order.

Capitalism and Democracy

From the late nineteenth century, capitalism and democracy appear to have moved along independent yet parallel paths. They gained in strength during the twentieth century, interacting mutually and establishing an interface. The result has been the welfare state, defining the role of the state in an interventionist manner. Following the Great Depression of the 1930s a more positive conception of the state was produced. Since then, the state began to be thought of as a means of correcting the imbalances of the capitalist order, making capitalism itself an agent of the liberal perspective on the state. In the process it gave a new lease of life to capitalism, this irony being the crux of the so-called Keynesian revolution. The latter has been interpreted in diverse ways. For some, democracy is perceived as no more than an occasional impediment to capitalist statecraft and its imperial-colonial spread round the world; while for others, (non-democrats such as Napoleon the Third in France, and the fascist and communist leaders of the twentieth century) capitalism, especially in its recent corporate version, grew rapidly when democracy was suspended than when it was in saddle.

In course of time, the intellectual debate led to political offshoots, starting with Western Europe and moving Southwards to the so-called developing countries. Indeed, it began to be seen, both in the thinking of Fabian-style intellectuals (from Beveridge to Keynes) and in class-based movements which put labour or social democratic parties in power and gave rise to social security states, that the very idea of integrating the welfare ethic into democratic theory could well pose a challenge to capitalism. Around the same time, marxist revolutions in major landmasses – the United Soviet Socialist Republic (USSR) and China being the catalysts of the widespread global phenomenon of the socialist challenge to capitalism – were also taking place. From this followed a growing coalition of forces, between the Soviet Union, other socialist countries and the leading powers of the third world, producing global formations like the Non-aligned Movement (NAM) and the G-77 in the United Nations.

Contrarywise, even with the power of the welfare ethic and global assertions from non-capitalist peripheries, democratic movements arising from global peripheries have not displaced capitalism. This was best illustrated by Allende's Chile— unaccompanied by an organised revolutionary movement democratic politics can at best be treated as an inconvenience that could well be contained by the capitalist political economy. Perhaps the same can be said about Nehru's India, Nyerere's Tanzania and Cardoso's Brazil. So long as inequitous and apartheidised civil societies rule the roost, democracy will prove incapable of undermining the power of capitalism. This has proved especially pertinent under the corporate capitalism of the late twentieth century. So long as the democratic state is structurally operating within the techno-economic framework of capitalism, irrespective of democracy's ideological intent to contain the capitalist threat, it is in reality found to be compatible with high degrees of inequality. Even the social security regimes are unable to stem the tides, both national and international, of capitalism. The key point of course is quite different: the crux of the idea of democracy lies in its invocation of concepts of dissent, resistance, exposure and liberty, with both individuals and communities asserting their unique configurations in the growth of a democratic social and ethical movement. None of the regimes we have discussed have been able to ensure such a movement.

Democracy as Myth

But while democracy is unable to defeat the aggressive logic of capitalism it continues to remain a living myth—in which large masses of the people have come to believe and in which national and international intelligentsia have placed their faith. Its great appeal is considered self-evident and obvious, not a matter for discussion, any more. Precisely because democracy is in the process of mythification that when questions are raised about its limits and contradictions, the answer given is that the world is going through a process of historical change, thus generating new challenges for democracy. The answer underscores the presence of democracy as a powerful myth. Following democracy's conversion into a myth almost everyone began claiming to be a democrat. As for the role of the west in this process, democracy started being exported as a value and a criterion of ethics, which was then scattered around the world. It encompassed a large number of nation states, cultures and civilisations, becoming in course of time a carrier of science and philosophy, of modern education, of development; contributing to the elaboration of themes like justice, exercise of power, engagement in thought and speech, declarations of equality and, through a number of conceptual steps, the birth of an at once empirical and normative science of politics. Democracy becomes a norm, and democratic politics a normative engagement, emphasising participation, transparency and accountability, leading to the full rhetoric of 'political science'.

Democracy and Legitimacy

In the west, since the French and American revolutions, a clear enunciation materialised—for a society to be truly modern, it has to be constitutional and democratic. The American Revolution added the thesis of self-determination to the democratic ideal. Only nation states were natural political entities, only they were permissible. The catchphrase was democratic national self-determination, with democracy and the nation state as two aspects of the modern incarnation. Moreover the concept of revolutionary rebirths, from the French and American revolutions to the nationalist revolutionary fervour in ex-colonial states and societies, provided the ideological thrust to the package of political transformations, and through them a reordering of societies leading to a composite framework based on nation states on the one hand and democracy on the other. The framework later received new inputs with the upsurges of the subaltern classes within national democratic societies.

Democratic Disappointments

While the idea of democracy has led to great expectations and has become a key point of political legitimacy, democracies – already established and those aspiring to be so – are in fact producing the greatest disappointments and frustrations of our times. A whole series of struggles has been waged throughout history and carried over to our own time period for the survival, defence and restoration of democracy. But it is democratic systems that have caused people the deepest disappointments.

In non-democratic systems there is neither the level of expectations found in democracies, nor the frustration and alienation associated with democracies. At various points of time and in many regions of the world there have emerged leaders and advocates of anti-democratic systems who have argued that socioeconomic results and even national security and national unity can better be achieved in the absence of democracy. On the whole, democracy is perhaps the most difficult system to establish and operate. It tends to be extremely fragile, often unstable, and open to unpredictable fluctuations. While democratic claims are becoming vital and necessary for achieving legitimacy, each democracy is found to encounter, at different phases in its evolution, some kind of crisis.

Contextualising Democracy

Placing democracy in a global context and within a socioeconomic framework, there seem to be two simultaneous tendencies at work: while the rich are found to be continuously engaged in excluding the poor and the middle strata of society, the poor are seeking to gain access to power and a degree of prosperity by engaging in the democratic political process. Or to state it obversely, the poor are found to be involved in opening up the democratic political process precisely at a time when the rich seem inclined to shut the doors of the system, impose iniquitous and aparthidised societies worldwide.

While there seems to have taken place a phenomenal increase in both inequity and apartheidisation, there is also a resurgence in democratic faith among the poor and the hitherto victimised. The democratic process – not just in India, but worldwide – is being impinged upon by two contradictory forces: a) democratic assertion of the subaltern classes, and b) the forces of globalisation reducing available democratic spaces. While the latter are turning more and more towards a technicised conception of both development and governance, the former appear determined to make poverty eradication an accepted social goal. The twentieth century has been a century of extremes with respect to both wealth and poverty. The failure of revolutions too is pushing the poor towards exclusion while the declared goal of human rights by western powers has tended to become an instrument to consolidate the corporate capitalist thrust of modernising societies. It is against this background and the accompanying discontent and despair that there is a growing demand in the Union Nations for making the twenty-first century the century of the poor. No doubt accepting this will call for a completely new revolution – a new conception of revolution altogether – in which democracy and human rights will become real catalysts of social transformation, with the poor themselves getting engaged in eradicating poverty.

Models of Democracy

The collapse of the Soviet Union, the post–cold war announcement of the 'end of history', and the consequent appeal for the spread of democracy and human rights round the world under the auspices of global elites appeared to enhance the prospects of democracy in large parts of the world. But a closer look at many of the functioning democracies leads to a different perception altogether. Important questions are being raised with regard to the authenticity and validity of the growth of democratic governance in a fast changing world.

A crucial aspect of the changes overtaking the world is the northward shift of power, resources and economic opportunities. Alongside the centralisation, internally, of power, resources and opportunities that has already taken place in large parts of the non-west (both in the third world and the former socialist world), civil societies and the world order face a fast-changing scenario. Meanwhile the challenges that had arisen from the grassroots of most societies are suffering fresh erosions, and the theoretical underpinnings of the critiques and challenges from the South have also witnessed lack of self-confidence. Democracy is more often contrasted with absence thereof than an actually realised standard in countries and domains where it is supposed to operate. It is expected to be more accountable to the people than other systems, and hence fulfilling minimum levels of justice and egalitarianism. But in practice quite often democracy by itself does not promote either equality or justice, only logical axioms like 'equality before law'. Instead it is found to live side by side with high levels of inequality, poverty in the midst of opulence, and ill-treatment of a wide variety of minorities for whom there is little by way of compensatory justice.

It is in this context that we need to evaluate the idea of representative democracy which has presumably become necessary with the growth in size and complexity of functions to be performed by governments and political systems. In fact, we have had a process of historical evolution that is in itself rather interesting: there has been movement from direct democracy provided by assemblies of small republics that prevailed in ancient systems of governance (for example, ancient Greece and ancient India) to systems of representation encompassing large territories, until both demands on governments and distances between the governors and the governed grew to the present point when once again there is a growing desire to move towards smaller and more spontaneous units. The trend is to decentralise, to move towards greater autonomy and self-rule, striving once again towards people ruling themselves in more rather than less direct forms of democracy.

Originally, in western theory, the idea of representative government was based on a combination of (a) the ancient ideal of egalitarianism interpreted as displacement of rulers by turn, and (b) the idea of a general will which slowly shifted from a general assembly of all adult citizens to electoral systems expressing the will of the people, which were presumed to act as mechanisms of control on the actions of politicians and bureaucrats. The justification for present-day representative governments is that given the reality of multi-interest and hence heterogeneous populations, it is the 'second best' approximation of the original idea (as was advanced by Schumpeter in his classical theory of democracy), perhaps better than any other system of government in present conditions. Increasingly, though, given the growing hold of autonomous bureaucracies, and transnational and corporate institutions, which have together depoliticised and rendered impotent citizens' own initiatives, it is becoming difficult to continue defending what remains of representative politics.

We may already be reaching the limits of representative democracy in our effort to bring about any real social change. For in reality we are witnessing a growing dichotomy between representation and participation-cum-citizenship. Direct democracy suggests a form of government in which all of the people are able to decide in all public matters, all of the time. Such a form could not be expected to function efficiently in modern, large scale, often continent-size nations with millions of citizens. Representative democracy has therefore emerged as a substitute for the purer forms of democracy, a form of democracy in which some of the people, presumably chosen by all, govern in all public matters, all of the time. This approach produced efficiency, but at enormous costs to participation and citizenship. Decentralised and self-rule oriented democracy tries to revitalise citizenship without wholly neglecting efficiency by defining democracy as a form of government in which all of the people govern themselves in at least some public matters, at least some of the time. In effect, representation is tied down to diverse interests, and as a result destroys participation and citizenship in general.

Democracy can survive only by striking roots in a direct form. It is secured not by great leaders but by competent, responsible citizens. We are free only as citizens, and our freedom and liberty are only as durable as our citizenship. Quoting Benjamin Barber, 'We may be born free but we die free only when we work at it in the interval between. And citizens are certainly not born, but made as a consequence of civic and political engagement in a free polity.' On representative democracy in this context he says, 'Representation destroys participation and citizenship even as it serves accountability and private rights.'

The Movement for Creating Emancipatory Democracy

With growing disillusionment with regard to prevailing models of democracy, in particular representative democracy, and the slowly emerging aspirations for what could be called genuine democracy (that is, direct democracy based on various degrees of self-rule, self-governance and self-determination), a newly inspired yearning for and expectation of transformative politics has materialised. Democracy could well become a legitimate instrument for transformative politics, based on an incipient movement for democracy, informed by an ethical imperative, leading individuals and societies towards world transformation. Provided, however, that there arises a new breed of democratic and human rights activists, to begin with from the core of an idealistic middle class, and then moving towards encompassing the people and their struggles in country after country, and ultimately the world as a whole. This will have to be just the opposite of the neo-liberal model of globalisation, producing instead an authentic global upsurge of peoples, communities, and ecologies; both drawing upon and at the same time moving beyond the so-called new social movements with regard to the environment, women, tribals, and deprived and disenfranchised castes and classes. This will be a movement that is deeply rooted in the *whole of civil society.*

10

On Democracy: Emancipation and Democracy

We have looked at an evaluation and critique of the prevailing theory of democracy, as well as the relevance of the idea of democracy to other values like freedom, justice, equity and self-determination; it would be worthwhile linking all these considerations into *one holistic thrust*, and engage in a search for one all-embracing concept and perception that will address a critical goal-oriented foci. Foci such as those involved in concepts like transformation, liberation, empowerment and emancipation. By moving towards such a broad and focussed perspective – both by delving deep in the terrain covered by democracy when it is fully realised, and by elevating from democracy and its institutional compass to something more normative and transformative – one is necessarily led to think in terms of an ever encompassing movement.

What prospects/possibilities are there for democracy and its institutional correlates to lead to people's emancipation/empowerment/liberation? As we have discussed in the previous chapter, democracy seems better equipped to impart legitimacy to elected regimes than to fulfil the basic aspirations of the people. For, ironic as it may sound, in and of itself, democracy has remained more an aspiration than a truly realised goal. How are we to conceptualise the idea of democracy? Do we conceptualise democracy as propelling a movement that produces diverse strands of transformative politics or simply as a framework of governance which then, failing to deliver the goods, leads to a variety of problems and frustrations, dilemmas and contradictions, which in turn call for a more comprehensive and socially widespread radical movement? The movement should work towards a truly radical and transformative orientation of the whole of civil society, as well as the polity, through a type of politicisation that goes to the roots of culture and civilisation. The movement should reach out to both individuals and communities, and grassroots and regional structures of governance. When one tries to think of democracy through the normative perspective of 'emancipation and democracy', and is in fact asking what diverse goals and values is a given democracy fulfilling, it is not merely about the issue of the nature of governance in that particular democracy or even governance in a generic sense. Because the conception of democracy has been narrow, it is producing a series of frustrations and problems. The emancipatory thrust of democracy calls for a change in its very definition and the diverse contents – social and cultural, local, national and global – through which it finds expression.

Is emancipation to be conceptualised as focussing mainly on the exploited and excluded strata? In my view emancipation needs to be conceived in holistic terms, reaching out from each individual (including individuals in the established social strata), to wider and wider circles of classes and communities. Emancipation should be a deeply rooted process of change, mobilisation and transformation. Emancipation is not a subject–object relationship in which some are emancipators and others are being emancipated. Either the whole society is emancipated, and with it every human being in it, or no one is. Those left out of the web of emancipation must suffer the consequences. To be left out also involves a state of being, of a condition characterised by alienation and anomie on which diverse philosophies (from existentialism to nihilism) and leading philosophers (from Weber to Durkheim) have dwelt at length, underscoring the deeper psycho-social states in which individuals and communities find themselves.

The Social Basis of Emancipation

Emancipation is at state of being which applies to all. It applies most of all to the middle class, which at one time was considered the torchbearer of freedom and autonomy. This means the idea of *swaraj* too needs to be conceived along with the political dimensions. The conception should be of an egalitarian restructuring of civil society, the uplifting of the *daridranarayan* and thereby moving towards a comprehensive model of equity, justice and emancipation.

But we seem to have moved away from such a holistic perspective. The reasons are our choice economic development and our attempt to catch up with the richer and more affluent countries. For the poorer classes and systems that have been left out of development, emancipation entails a call for a major ideological remodelling towards transformative politics, economics, environment and culture.

Ideological Restructuring

Seen from such a variety of thresholds the ethics of emancipation necessarily leads to a major shift in ideas, institution building and political engagement—the three together providing a powerful normative thrust, almost a catharsis of the human community as a whole. The catharsis could range from individual selves to community structures, to national and international alignments of both structural and ideological kinds.

The ideological challenge is probably the most pervasive and multidimensional of all. We happen to be facing a major intellectual, and hence ideological, vacuum. Neither the liberal nor the marxist, nor even the Gandhian conception provides us with a workable model of fundamental change, though each did strive to provide one. For change to be truly far reaching and fundamental, one needs to dwell deep into the psychic, existential and soul-searching arenas of human striving. Not long ago a combination of these three or four streams – interacting with each other and mutually reinforcing and questioning each other – did provide a workable framework of development, growth and structural refashioning. The framework also made it possible for human communities to take on ever new challenges from a whole variety of sources. Today it seems possible neither to comprehend in which direction change should be undertaken nor to make social and political choices that can lead to transformative processes.

How then are we to move out of such a stagnant pool? Is it even possible to conceive of a course of action, some kind of a movement away from where we are currently positioned? To the extent we can conceive of such a course of action, will it be possible to indicate the concrete steps involved in undertaking such a course of action? The course of action should involve a theoretical conception of the future and on that basis work towards a practical refashioning of the human effort that will, in effect, be ideological. It should also involve a restructuring of the sociopolitical discourse undertaken within a systemic framework.

Such a conception of an ideological challenge would inspire a stirring of human consciousness among all political strata, in particular among the marginalised and victimised. The challenge should ultimately help build an emancipatory ethic—emancipation of the whole of society and then the world. This will involve taking into its purview the whole series of problems humankind is encountering—poverty, inequity, injustice and the erosion of natura resources; and their ethnic, ecological and civilisational dimensions.

Poverty, Democracy and Emancipation

In dealing with poverty one is up against an inequitous, unjust and increasingly polarised social order. The polarisation consists of a minority of the privileged and a vast majority of the deprived and the destitute. It is a polarisation with respect to maintaining minimum standards of living—health, shelter, education, access to the environment and other such basics. Larger and larger numbers of people are excluded from the mainstream of the society and driven into ghettos. They are now described as constituting the unorganised sector of migrating humans and animals, clusters of refugees, women and children. We live in an unemancipated society consisting of diverse social segments, species and environments.

There cannot be genuine emancipation without a just and egalitarian state of existence. It is not only the basic social order that should exist in an egalitarian state, but also the vast diversity of its ethnic, biological and ecological components. The very mention of democracy in this overall context of existence should involves – especially in a society like India with an almost total absence of the democratic ethos – social, political, cultural, ecological and bio-ethnic infrastructures. There can be no real democracy without an emancipated social order and a free and fulsome diversity of natural resources.

The Democratic Facet

If this then be the freshly conceived and comprehensive, multifaceted idea of democracy, we should also pose an obverse query of the same theme: Is democracy a sufficient instrument of emancipation? Democracy may require an emancipatory thrust and that too in a multicultural framework. But what about democracy itself, in its relation to human emancipation? How far are the two to be interfaced, and in what precise structure? What is prior? Which is to be given primacy? Or is this an ideal question? Should we at all pose it? And if we do, what role and position is democracy to assume in that interface?

This may well be the point at which we have to raise a few pertinent issues vis-à-vis democracy. First, democracy ought not be merely conceived in constitutional-cum-political terms, pertaining only to governance. It involves wider dimensions—achievement of justice, assertion of freedom, high degree of tolerance and acceptance of diversity. And in each of these dimensions, apart from the political aspect, the sociocultural, bio-ethnic and ecological aspects should also be considered. Democracy needs to be conceived within a holistic framework of reference. Democracy is bound to fail as an instrument of emancipation if a multifaced perspective is not employed.

Second, the wider the distance between the elites and the peoples, between those who govern and the governed, the less the extent of democracy and less emancipated the structure of governance. Therefore, less emancipation with regard to development, culture, ecology and ethnicity. In the times we live in, these distances are setting apart governing elites, developmental superstructures, cultural academies and councils, natural resource endowments, and federal and multinational bodies from their local, confederal, grassroots and supposedly decentralised units. Technologies – hardware and software, from genetic to information technologies – have streamrolled levels and estates, core structures and networks, superstructures and so-called bases.

Third, built in the frameworks of functioning democracies are self-imposed distances – from constitutional to political, socioeconomic to administrative – which engineer growing dissensions, ever-widening divisions and yawning top–down gaps. These produce alienation, widening disparities and cultures of impairment between the centres and the peripheries, and quite often along the way regional substructures and subcultures. The world we live in is a world of eroding self-governance, autonomy and decentralised units of identity and self-definition. No doubt, it is also a world in which countervailing tendencies are on the rise. We are witnessing major upsurges of consciousness among the hitherto suppressed and victimised strata. An activist agenda is at work. The marginalised and underprivileged also want to engage themselves in arenas of action, whether through the ongoing electoral and representative processes, or through more direct participation structures of self-governance and developmental hierarchies. They are also seeking positions in educational institutions, administrative units, and economic and cultural entities.

The Arena of Power and Influence

Countervailing tendencies are at work, though they still remain in the realm of aspirations and expectations. Much of what is desired has not yet been realised, not at any rate in full measure. Even seemingly symbolic measures like reservations for the scheduled caste and scheduled tribes, later extended to other backward castes, and sought after for women, have begun to move hitherto wholly excluded sections into diverse arenas of power and influence. This has produced a great deal of resistance from established elites, quite often leading to outbursts of violence and repression. These counterattacks are being recognised and in turn countered through diverse measures of rebuttal and reverse frames of action, often, in fact, forcing the elites to accomodate and accept. The *senas* let loose by the upper castes in Bihar and Andhra Pradesh are met with powerful counter-armies and movements such as the mazdoor kisan sangharsh samitis. All of it leading to networks of solidarity and consciousness raising, producing actual counterforce against the status quo. Much of this is being currently conceived both by those directly involved in mounting these upsurges and more generally by conscientious segments of the middle classes and the media. As yet there is no assurance that the populations inhabiting these conscientious sections are growing. There is little doubt that a fresh infusion of ideas as well as institutional expressions are growing. The objective conditions that nurture them are already there. A mutual interface between objective conditions and creative assertions vis-à-vis those conditions also seems to be happening; not necessarily everywhere – in all societies and at all levels – and yet on a rising curve of both potentiality and possibility.

The status quo is intact. The cracks are are still of a transitional kind, yet to indicate a clear direction with a lasting imprint. The transitions however have clearly begun to make themselves felt. Something new seems to be in the offing. But it is not certain. It cannot be easily wished away or put down as a mere dream of utopia. We are at least at the crossroads, even though the path on which we are likely to traverse is as yet uncertain.

The Era of Uncertainty

It is this condition of uncertainty that characterises our age and era that needs to be gauged, bearing in mind its diverse manifestations. I have tried to gauge this condition in my work on the political process in India; on globalisation and the neo-liberal framework of ideas that informs it; and on the specific dimensions of reality impinging on the political economy and the aura of security (with reference the growth of national security states). These are getting intertwined with chauvinist conceptions of both the nation state and the international order. I have argued that the two together are producing a model of secular fundamentalism of the modernist variety (to be distinguished from the fundamentalism of the communal, religious and casteist varieties). I am not a believer of the antimodernist or postmodernist conception of the human predicament. I see value in aspects of tradition and the indigenous roots of our existence as peoples, civil societies and states. But I am not inclined to be overtaken by the myth of switching from an undefined and undifferentiated modernity to a sweeping idea of an equally undefined and undifferentiated tradition.

All these make for a notion of uncertainty full of ambivalences, ambiguities, pitfalls, dilemmas and growing contradictions. We seem unable to deal with it. For it is not just an era of uncertainty, but an *aura* of uncertainty that we need to grasp and unravel.

However, this is not the first time that the human race has been up against an aura of uncertainty. Quite often in the past there have been periods of acute uncertainty. When the age of empires gave place to a world of nation states, there was a period of uncertainty. It is by no means clear that the Treaty of Westphalia ushered in the nation state phenomenon—an excessively technocratic and militaristic interpretation of modern history. Far more important was the combination of (a) the growth of linguistic nationalism following the end of the Napoleonic era, (b) the rise of the German nation on the ruins of the Austro-Hungarian empire and the diplomacy of Metternich, (c) imperialist expansion following the successful growth of the Industrial Revolution, and (d) the neo-imperial rise of Franco-German, Franco-British and Franco-Russian rivalries. Still later, following the Congress of Vienna, there was the rise of aggressive German nationalism ending in two major wars. At the end of the second of these wars, there was a rise of new nationalisms in the hitherto non-politicised and non-militarised continents of the world. The story of the rise and decline of nationalism worldwide in the wake of the anticolonial struggles in the continents of the South needs to be imaginatively grasped if we are to understand and then overcome the uncertainty that the world has faced ever since.

Next in line, in chronological time, comes an uncertainty not born out of geopolitics, but rather due to the denial of geopolitics, even its rationale. Instead, the world has been overtaken by the realm of ideas in action—a succession of revolutionary upsurges. First the French Revolution, then the American Revolution, and after a lapse of more than a century the Russian and the Chinese revolutions. They were followed by the Vietnamese revolution and a whole series of partly nationalist, partly socioeconomic upsurges of human emancipation. Most of these were located in the global South; there emerged a coalition of socialist and nationalist formations, together mounting a comprehensive resistance to the global status quo, imperial hegemonies, and in many of these countries, authoritarian and neo-fascist regimes. Simultaneously there took place a challenge to centralised governments and anti-people syndromes of policies, development models and structures of hegemony. Over the centuries revolutions have produced massive anticlimaxes and highly frustrating degenerations, leading in course of time to major erosions in the very heart of the human spirit. Though somehow the latter has been kept alive through periodic infusions of optimism, it has also been subject to traumas of certainty turning into massive uncertainty. Particularly in the twentieth century, many illusions have collapsed—national sovereignty; the once-inspiring coalition of socialist and third-worldist ideals; the Soviet alternative; later still in the post–cold war phase, the Gorbachev-inspired era of peace and disarmament. And within mixed economies and polities, the erosion of the left. Taking advantage of these various erosions, the neo-liberal offshoot of the unipolar, hegemonic American reality has risen to power.

The Dialectic

There is need to delve deeper into the dialectic of certainty and uncertainty. For in each of the historical moments where the aura of uncertainty finally emerged, there was, and that too for a long time, a belief in *certainty*.

Let us briefly examine this before concluding this section on the growth of uncertainty in human affairs. The dialectic could be a result of the steady undermining of the medieval order of princelings and feudal lords, and the entry of the modern age of technologies and nation states; or the industrial growth after the enclosures of vast hinterlands of agriculture and rural crafts; or the gradual crystallisation of geopolitical entities backed by military-strategic power; or the product of inevitable conflicts between rival centres of power that emerged from the very logic of geopolitics; or the whole thrust of political economy starting with the Industrial Revolution and then its imperialist spread worldwide; or the gradual intermeshing of the political and techno-economic arms of the modern system producing the modern imperial era and resulting in wars and revolutions. The consequent degeneration of one set of states and nations and regeneration of another set of societies, produced fresh stirrings in the human edifice, ending in our era of growing ambiguities, dilemmas, contradictions and uncertainties. At no point was there an inevitable growth of uncertainty. At each stage there was a feeling of confidence and certainty among the principal actors on the scene. But at every point new tendencies were surfacing, new actors emerging and new churnings taking place in diverse sociopolitical spaces. These elements first arose in the realm of consciousness and then in that of action, producing in our minds a sense of uncertainty.

This trajectory of diverse strands of fairly confident feelings about reality confronts us and leads us to a series of dialectics. Because the dialectics were not permitted to smoothly work themselves out, they produce in our minds a sense of growing uncertainty.

Positive Thinking

The human species faces a set of uncertainties. But a state of uncertainty does not necessarily amount to a state of despair, an end to all hope and the acceptance of an uncertain future. A state of uncertainty only pronounces a lack of clear affirmation of hope about the prospects for humanity and its future. By no means does it pronounce a determined or irreversible state of affairs. Indeed, a state of uncertainty could be taken up as a challenge to regain and reaffirm hope. Uncertainty could be seen as a challenge to both imagination and praxis, and towards conceiving a better prospect for both imagination and praxis. If the march of history is full of uncertainties, it is equally full of initiatives towards new openings of the historical process. It could lead to an opening out towards a new and positive reality, and an alternative to both the present and the past. A state of uncertainty could well prove to be a catalytic moment, a stepping stone towards a genuine utopia, a conception of something that has never existed before, even in periods of great confidence and hope. Fortunes and potentialities have been reversed. But that very process may also be seen as calling for a fundamental change—precisely what the dawn of uncertainty made possible.

Implications for Emancipation and Democracy

We have dwelt at some length on the phenomenon of uncertainty in dealing with the human predicament only to comprehend the import of it for the larger theme of emancipation and democracy. We have highlighted issues and challenges that have emerged, the contradictions and failures as of now, and the possible ways out of the very crisis of transformative politics vis-à-vis civil society at home and the global context at large. The coexistence of and correlation of democracy and emancipation is what makes the future appear uncertain though, as already stated, that very uncertainty could well become a catalyst of new initiatives and alternatives for the social order and its deeper psycho-cultural and ecological – and of course, political – underpinnings. It is precisely this situation of opposing tendencies and possibilities that makes it incumbent on the still ambivalent and drifting intelligentsia to rise to the occasion and engage in a movement for democratic resurgence. The engagement should work towards a comprehensive social and ethical transformation. Without such transformation, resurgence is impossible to achieve.

Democracy has remained a dream and an aspiration. As a system it has not been realised in practice. But the aspiration is very much alive, both in the conscientious sections of the educated and thinking class and, in fact even more, in the deprived and dispossessed sections of the population. The latter continue to face backlashes from the dominant strata, and are often forced to join streams of militancy and violence. But the aspirations continue to challenge both the mass public and the visionary segments of the as yet unclear and ambivalent intelligentsia. Together the masses and the intelligentsia, could engage in a diversity of struggles.

The challenge before the intelligentsia is to keep alive this flame of hope and resurgence, and to continue offering ideological alternatives to the struggling segments of the mass public. While the latter consists of segments – dalits, tribals, women, aspiring youth – that are to be the principal authors of the slowly emergent movement for democracy and emancipation, there will still be need for a democratic and human rights constituency consisting of activists, intellectuals and a whole array of individuals and communities committed to civil liberties. Drawing on the micro and intermediate thresholds, thousands are at work to ensure macro systemic change, giving rise to an all-India – and global – platform whose calls and appeals will mobilise the entire activist arena.

11

Conclusion: Democracy under Contrary Pressures

We have looked at how the vast diversity that characterises Indian democracy gets mobilised in moving from micro and intermediate spaces to macro transformation. Let us now consider the macro and micro dimensions together impinging on the functioning of the polity. The two have shifted from being complementary to contradictory pressures on liberal democracy—globalisation on the one hand, and decentralisation and grassroots upsurges on the other.

Democracy

With globalisation, in the name of spreading democracy and human rights around the world, we are in fact witnessing a consolidation of the capitalist framework. Capitalism has shifted from the earlier imperial and colonial framework to an essentially corporatist framework, consisting of the Brettonwoods institutions, and the transnational and multinational corporations. Ideologically the shift involves a redefinition of democracy, particularly liberal democracy, towards what has been called the neo-liberal framework of liberalisation, globalisation and privatisation. Also involved is trouble for the nation state, particularly in the third world countries, as well as moving from a capitalism based on the market within each country to that based on world capital. The erosion of the welfare state followed the decline of the market in the democratic and liberal sense, with the movement towards a model of capitalism based on a hegemonic conception of that world.

Following the collapse of the Soviet Union, there has been considerable interest in adopting democratic forms, party frameworks and a more consumer-oriented economic model in the formerly socialist countries of the world. The notion of spreading democracy and human rights is not restricted to the developing countries of the third world, but extends to the formerly socialist countries. A new world order – the term coined by the then American president George Bush Sr – based on the neo-liberal ideological framework was emerging. The presumption about the neo-liberal framework of development and democracy is that it will provide a new post-statist model of freedom, democracy, liberty, etc. Instead of emphasising the sovereignty of diverse nation states and their role in providing welfare-oriented notions, and of the accountability that states hold vis-à-vis civil societies, we are offered a new framework of governance—globalisation; and a new ideological perspective—neo-liberalism. Both together undercut and ultimately undermine the role of the state.

Communalism and Democracy

A new face of democracy is being advanced in countries like India and Pakistan—communalism. We are seeing a convergence of the communal, fundamentalist majoritarian view and the neo-liberal ideology. The marketised model of globalisation and dominance, and the fundamentalist model of a communal type are converging to form a new framework of democracy. According to the Weberian framework two apparently contradictory trends cannot unfold at the same time. But having a competitive, liberal, liberalising or neo-liberal model, and simultaneously, communal tensions in the country, is contradictory.

Economic Reforms and Democracy

Indian democracy is not only facing an erosion as a result of the communal pressures building from below, but also because of the spate of economic reforms which have done major damage to the democratic process. The reforms were launched in 1991, with the new economic programme under the joint stewardship of Prime Minister Narsimha Rao and Finance Minister Manmohan Singh. India continued more or less in the same direction, the transnational structures being made more welcome under the auspices of the National Democratic Alliance. The emerging combination of pressures and policies have led to considerable growth in inequity and unemployment. There is also growing evidence of stagnation in the agricultural sector.

Integrating Indian economy into the world market necessarily means leaving behind large sections of the society, excluding them from the purview of economic development and perceiving them as dispensable. Sometimes there may be pangs of conscience or embarrasment among some due to the continuing growth in the number of the poor in the country. But the pangs quieten down soon.

The Growth of Inequality

India is also facing a decline in the role of the organised sector, of industrial and technological growth – textile, steel, machine goods and consumer industries – catering both to local needs and for exports. There has been considerable growth in the unorganised sector. While the 1990s had a relatively high rate of growth and were assumed to have produced a considerable transformation of the economy, it was also the decade when poverty was on the increase, rural development had been undercut, small and independent entrepreneurs were forced to close down, and handicrafts and cottage industries were not keeping pace with the other segments of the economy. It is in this time frame that corporate capitalism had been on the upswing with growing entry of transnational and multinational corporations concentrating on the hi-tech sectors. Recent research has revealed that within the so-called middle-class market it is only the tip of the iceberg of modern technology that is being sought after by the multinational corporations. Their focus on the high tech industries and underestimation of the growing middle class along with the lower classes, is further reinforcing the dichotomy between the rich and the super rich on the one hand, and the middle and the lower classes on the other. There is a tremendous obsession with the rich and the super rich, which is seen by the media to be an indicator of prosperity. Large sections of the working class and the lower castes and communities are being excluded and retrenched. Additionally there is the phenomenon of segments of the middle class also getting pauperised, as a result of the transnational strategies being pursued.

Globalisation

With regard to the phenomenon of globalisation, we have to deal with a highly complex reality. Though globalisation appeals to the elite strata as the only process at work, in the citadels of capitalism, globalisation is actually weakening. There are trade wars between the US and Japan, and major differences are emerging between the US and the European Union. They seem to have different positions within the United Nations on issues like Yugoslavia, Bosnia and Somalia. Globalisation is going strong in large parts of the third world, where the governments are being seduced by the corporatist model and the neo-liberal doctrine of development.

Even in parts of the third world, globalisation is being challenged. Opposition to western domination and criticism of the global economic policy is increasing in the Islamic world; in China; in the democratic revolutions gradually taking place in countries like Indonesia; among the dissident democratic minorities in Burma, Tibet and the Chiapas region of Mexico; and in Malaysia. Countries like India are in the thrall of the phenomenon of globalisation despite the criticism levelled against it. As a consequence, the media pays greater attention to trade, investments, balance of payments and foreign exchange reserves rather than to poverty and unemployment. By following a particular framework of development, we have increased the feelings of alienation and disenchantment among the mass of the people. But people are also beginning to take advantage of the democratic process to resist the imposition of the economic reforms and the consolidation of the corporate sector.

There is a fair amount of opposition to globalisation though it is being supported by a strong conceptual and ideological framework. Neither the earlier conception of liberalism, nor marxism, nor the Gandhian framework are holding out against the more recent neo-liberal framework urging movement towards corporate capitalism. This framework, though recent, seems to have succeeded in rolling back all other ideological thinking.

Decentralisation

The new version of capitalism and the appeal of neo-liberalism to elite structures has resulted in the alienation of the people vis-à-vis the socioeconomic framework, the political system and transnational corporations. It is leading to more conflicts between the dominant castes and communities vis-à-vis the formal democratic process. We have hung parliaments and legislatures. This underscores increasing levels of discontent in the life chances of the individual, the community, the family and the neighbourhood. The people are in search of ways in which they can fall back on their own resources, natural and political, and for an alternative to the general framework of parliamentary democracy and the globalising structure of development and governance.

This search is leading to a growing revulsion against the centralised state structure and the globalised framework of policies and politics. It is from the search that a decentralised model of the state is emerging. It is a model that respects diversity and is pluralistic. This model promotes self-rule rather than an individualised notion of democracy based on majority and minority rules. We have had a situation in which the bottom of the system was coopted into the top–down framework of parliamentary democracy and bureaucratic rule. But as a result the communities at the bottom are asserting their control of their own natural resources and their capacity to govern themselves. Thus decentralisation works contrary to globalisation; decentralisation in terms of self-rule, with citizens in control of institutions of governance.

There are problems inherent even in the decentralised alternative. The mere conception of decentralised development and governance, particularly of the panchayati raj type, is not going to provide solutions. In the 1950s, following the community development experience which led to a fair amount of bureaucratic control, the Balwant Rai Mehta Committee was appointed. The committee proposed that there should be people's control over the institutions of development and came forward with the conception of the panchayati raj. From the time of the committee to that of the 72nd and 73rd constitutional amendments which required states to hold elections for panchayati raj bodies, we have travelled a long way in building the institutions of the panchayati raj. Why is it that despite so much effort and so much thought being given to panchayati raj institutions, that governance has not necessarily satisfied the expectations of the people? Is it because in reality there is no assurance that the political leadership will permit people's participation at the grassroot levels? There has been a great deal of debate on the role of deprived groups, particularly on the role of women, and on the new legislation that has taken place at the panchayat and zilla parishad levels, which has empowered the truly deprived communities. We are now being how and why achievements at the panchayat level must be implemented at the state and national levels.

The Switch from Centralisation to Decentralisation

Let us examine the almost sudden switch that has taken place from hope in a centralised system of government to a contrary hope in a decentralised model of governance. Decentralisation is expected to usher less corruption, less exploitation, less discrimination and so on. With some outstanding exceptions, all we have is a large array of institutions at many levels, quite often crisscrossing and overlapping, producing a series of dyarchies – decentralisation translated as panchayati raj – that were supposed to transfer power to the people, but have been unsuccessful. In most of the states power is decentralised in certain respects, leading to a greater access to resources. Though there are additional provisions meant to promote various measures of self-rule, there have been no major transformations.

The changes that have taken place, though numerous, are scattered; and they are essentially at micro-levels or are confined to a few regions. Very few successful experiments that have been carried out. Not much thought has been given to simultaneously transforming the *macro*-system. We have lost faith in what used to be such a system—the Nehruvian model of democracy.

Communities now want to control and protect their access to natural resources, and thereby protect the great diversity of crops and seeds, and agricultural yields. These communities are becoming more and more aware that forests are being denuded and that water resources are fast declining. It is this new combination of concern for environmental and natural resource issues and concern for self-rule in governance that is giving rise to the notion of biodiversity. Diversity is not only conceived in sociopolitical terms, in terms of pluralism in the political arena, but is also considered on the biological and ecological fronts. The result is biodiversity, latest frontier of the struggle for a diversified and true democratic order.

We still need to admit, that all this is still taking place at a micro-level and that the situation at the macro-level continues to be relatively stagnant. The interest in preserving the diversity of agricultural produce and seeds is certainly leading to a conception of biodiversity, which had already begun with the changing conception of access to natural resources, as well as with what is taking place in the sociopolitical arena. And to that extent, the effort has not remained at the micro-level, it has moved to the intermediate level. One hopes that as more and more of these efforts succeed, it will make other communities also strive for similar transformation.

Towards an Environmental Perspective

If the situation in which we seem to be placed is still highly localised, it only calls for further efforts in the direction in which environmentalists are moving. Greater emphasis is being placed on the role of communities located in bio-regions wanting to preserve their crops and seeds. These are communities that are becoming aware of what is happening to the forests and water resources around them. There is a fair amount of hope that transformation will take place.

The problem lies in the sudden and radical shift from belief in the centralised model to faith in decentralisation, starting with panchayati raj, and moving towards local communities exercising control over resources. Perhaps there is a need to be skeptical about the new faith. To assume that merely by providing leadership and opportunities to local communities will mean an end to exploitation is romantic. It would produce ideal communities here and there, but would not necessarily bring about basic change in society. We definitely need to move in the direction of self-rule, of communities in control of natural resources, of decentralisation. But at the same time we must try our best to handle the macro-situation and initiate a process of transformation. We cannot rely entirely either on the centralised or the decentralised model. The presumption that virtue lies only in one level and not in all others should be questioned.

I recommend that we undertake both types of change simultaneously. We think in terms of transformation of the macro-system, in India in South Asia, in the third world, and in the world at large. In short, we should pursue a simultaneous process of transformation, at both the macro-level and micro-level, both the national and international levels, first within individual nations and civil societies, and then move towards globalised spaces.

The Need for a Macro-perspective

Globalisation needs to be countered, not just with decentralised and regional alternatives, or new initiatives with regard to natural resources and ecology, but also with political and ecological initiatives at the national, regional and global levels. The last should be conceptualised in terms of the international political economy and global ecology, and also by politically restructuring the prevailing world order. In my own work and thought, I have tried, through the concept of the non-party political process, to bring together social-action-oriented work at local levels and academic work in national and the international arenas. I continue to pursue this mode of thinking.

We have entered a phase of human history in which globalised structures will continue to prevail—globalised policies, resource endowments, technological knowhows and institutional models. Yet we want to move away from the hegemonic design of the so-called new world order that the US had put forward. We need to make efforts simultaneously at all levels in changing priorities, and emphasising certain principles and ideological nuances; but at no point should the hegemonic structure remain unchallenged.

I have attempted to articulate a diverse, complex, multilevel and multicultural agenda, thereby concluding the arguments used to rethink the whole democratic enterprise. I hope to reach out to a wide-ranging assembly of thinkers and doers. I continue to pursue this agenda of transformative politics, and social and cultural emancipation. I invite all thinking activists to join in that effort—thinkers engaging with the historical process and intellectuals-cum-activists intervening at critical points in the agenda of human action. In sum, human emancipation should be conceived in broad and comprehensive terms. The means, permeated by emancipatory goals, should be at once intellectual and activist. The arenas of emancipation should range from social change in institutional and ideological terrains to the more fundamental areas of ethics and philosophy.